Interest Rate Swaps

A Self-Study Guide to Mastering and Applying Interest Rate Swaps

Coopers
& Lybrand

IRWIN
Professional Publishing®
Chicago • London • Singapore

First published by IFR Publishing, London, UK, 1992/1993

ISBN 1-55738-589-0

Printed in the United States of America

BB

5 6 7 8 9 0

Contents

Preface

Since its inception in the early 1980s the swaps market has experienced phonomenal growth and is now a market of over US$3 trillion in size. This exponential growth means that swaps are now used by most financial institutions and corporate treasuries. At present there are only 70 swaps houses recognised by the International Swaps Dealers Association (ISDA)—largely major players in the international capital markets. Yet, as demand for these products continues to increase, the market will surely experience further growth in both the size and in the number of players. Innovation in the marketplace may be dominated currently by a few sophisticated derivatives houses, but many more organizations are involved in the day-to-day activity.

A professional guide to understanding swaps is essential for the various participants—be they management, trainee traders, back office support, system designers, accountants, or corporate treasurers seeking to use swaps in asset management. The Workbook Series on Derivatives is an excellent and muchneeded contribution to helping those with an interest in swaps to understand the variety and complexity of today's market.

John S. Spences
Deputy Chief Executive
Barclays de Zoete Wedd
November 1992

Foreword

In October 1991 we published *The Financial Jungle—a guide to financial instruments* to help promote the understanding of financial instruments and to identify the risks and benefits to both designers and users. Our sponsorship of the Workbook Series on Derivatives continues this theme.

New, increasingly sophisticated and complex swaps products are being designed all the time. The pace of change has been so rapid that many supporting personnel as well as senior management have struggled to keep step with the risk, accounting, tax, and regulatory implications of these innovative products. Examples abound on what happens when organizations trade financial instruments without fully understanding how they are put together.

It is vital that the designers understand the accounting and tax implications of the financial instruments they are seeking to promote. Equally, it is important for the users of instruments to comprehend their economic rationale and effect to ensure all risks are identified before transactions are completed. We believe these workbooks are part of the answer. They are well structured and easy to follow guides on how swaps are designed and how they work. Divided into four volumes—*Interest Rate Swaps, Currency Swaps, Equity Swaps, and Swaps and Financial Engineering*—they are invaluable study aids.

Phil Rivett
Chairman, Securities and Commodities Group

Paul Reyniers
Chairman, Financial Risk Management Group

Coopers & Lybrand
November 1992

Introduction

It is not an exaggeration to say that the interest rate swap constitutes the most important financial innovation of the last decade. Many other new instruments emerged to great acclaim (by their innovators at least). However, most have been responses to specific circumstances, typically tax and regulatory distortions, and their popularity waned once their particular window of opportunity closed. Swaps, on the other hand, have proved to be a fundamental and lasting development and are now in general and routine use throughout the financial sector, supported by a vast and still rapidly-growing market.

Swaps perform a number of key functions:

■   arbitrage between markets — between the money market and the capital market, between different sectors of the money market, between different currencies, and with other derivative instruments: by exchanging payments between markets, swaps have played a crucial role in the integration and globalisation of the financial markets, improving the efficiency of financial intermediation and providing borrowers with cheaper funds and investors with higher returns.

■   risk management: the exchange of interest payments through swaps allows the unbundling of the various features of funding and investment instruments (eg, the separation of interest and currency risk from the source of funding) and the financial engineering of these features into synthetic or repackaged instruments, often in combination with other derivative instruments.

■   gaining access to markets: where borrowing or lending is blocked by regulation, illiquidity, general underdevelopment, investor resistance, or any other obstacle, the exchange of payments through swaps provides access to the interest rates and currency of that market without the need to fund or invest in it.

Swaps emerged as instruments to exploit new issue arbitrage opportunities between the money and capital markets, and they remain a key factor in the primary market in international bonds: it is estimated that between one-half and three-quarters of new international bond issues are swapped. However, increasing availability and liquidity have promoted swaps as an essential instrument in routine risk management and this has been reflected in growing corporate use. The use of swaps has also been extended through greater recognition of their similarities with other derivatives such as FRAs, futures and options. The related development of hybrid derivatives, particularly through the combination of swaps and options, the application of swaps to physical commodities and equities, and the entry into the swap market of new intermediaries such as insurance companies, has also contributed to this growth.

The success of swaps is illustrated by the dramatic growth of the market. From negligible volumes in 1980, the market — in terms of the notional principal amount of new swaps — reached the equivalent of some US$923bn in the first half of 1991. Of this, single-currency interest rate swaps accounted for some US$762bn. At end-June 1991, the total notional principal amount of outstanding swaps exceeded the equivalent of US$2,889bn, of which single-currency interest rate swaps accounted for US$2,312bn. The exponential trend is illustrated in the table below.

US$bn	New swaps		All outstanding swaps (end period)
	All swaps	Interest rate swaps	
1981	3*	n/a	
1982	10*	n/a	
1983	45*	40*	
1984	70*	60*	
1985	100*	80*	
1986			
1987		683	
1988		1,010	
1989		1,503	
1990	1,477	1,264	
1991	923	762	2,889

Source: ISDA (from 1987)
* Das, Swap Financing

Swaps have also become available in an increasingly wider range of currencies. Initially, the market was concentrated in US dollars. This remains the largest sector but there are now liquid markets in at least 16 currencies. The distribution of the interest rate swap market by currency in the first half of 1991 is illustrated in the pie chart opposite.

The success of swaps is not just a quantitative matter. Indeed, the growth of the swap market has only been possible because of greater qualitative sophistication. The emergence of market-makers, who underpin liquidity, would not have occurred without the innovation of risk techniques such as warehousing and portfolio management. There has also been an improvement in the general understanding of swap risk, which in turn has led to greater confidence among the intermediaries who absorb those risks.

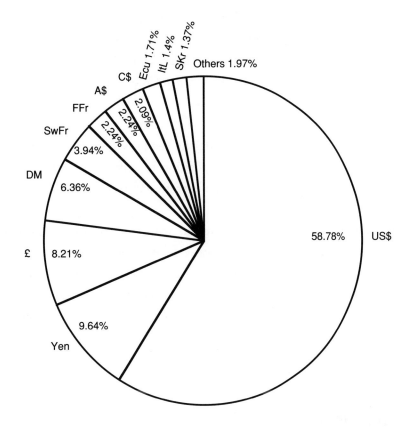

The growth of swaps has inevitably thrown up the sort of structural problems that affect all maturing markets: intensified competition and increased overheads resulting in reduced margins for intermediaries; the entry of lesser credits; the increase in the general risk exposure of market-makers; the constraints and uncertainties of the legal framework. Nevertheless, despite the UK local authority fiasco, the swaps market so far remains relatively free of regulatory wranglings. This partly reflects the market's own efforts, under the aegis of the International Swap Dealers Association (ISDA). In particular, ISDA has produced standardised contract documentation and continues to promote the concepts of netting and assignability.

There is however a limit to internal progress. The effective general default by the UK local authorities was, in large part, the product of regulatory and legal confusion rather than a market failure. Legal uncertainties have also undermined ISDA's attempts to persuade the banking supervisors to relax the capital adequacy requirements on swaps. The market has also been affected by general concerns over the creditworthiness of counterparties as the world's major economies entered recession at the end of the 1980s. One direct consequence has been the retreat of many of the US banks which pioneered swaps. The gap has not been completely filled by banks from other countries and liquidity has therefore been affected.

The swap market has a number of other challenges to address, not least of which is the inevitable deceleration in growth as the market continues to mature. However, there is little doubt that swaps have shown tremendous staying power and are now a permanent feature of the financial markets. A good understanding of them must therefore be an essential requirement for anyone involved in the financial markets.

The purpose of this self-study workbook is to provide the reader with a thorough grounding in interest rate swaps. From this, the reader will be in a position to talk confidently and credibly to other market practitioners. The workbook also bridges the current gap in swaps literature at this level.

Those intending to use this workbook should be familiar with basic interest rate concepts and arithmetic, including forward-forward interest rates. However, unnecessary complications in the guise of alternative interest rate conventions (ie, differences in day counts and annual bases), in compounding and in coupon payment frequencies are omitted. Knowledge of these conventions is vital when trading or using swaps, but has been left to one side here because they are not specific to swaps and are widely available from other sources.

How to use this workbook

The workbook is designed as a self-study programme. It has therefore been structured to guide the reader systematically through the subject and provides practical examples and case studies throughout to illustrate key points. The sources of market information used by experienced swaps practitioners are summarised and examples have been included from both screen-based information services and market publications.

A set of questions and answers is provided at the end of each section to enable the reader to test and monitor progress. To further facilitate the planning of study time, an estimate for the time needed to complete each chapter and set of exercises is given. Instructions for marking the exercises are set out at the back of the workbook. Both the timing and marking system are based on actual tests given to a representative sample of readers.

The workbook has been designed primarily for those with little or no experience of swaps, particularly where there is an urgent need to know. Experienced swap dealers and sales staff, however, may also find it valuable, not only in organising the training of their junior staff, but also when making swaps presentations to clients who require a degree of familiarisation with the subject.

Other workbooks in the series:

Currency Swaps
Equity Swaps
Swaps and Financial Engineering

For further information on the workbook series, please call Probus Publishing at 1-800-PROBUS-1 or 1-312-868-1100.

1 The swap mechanism

What is an interest rate swap?

Definition	An interest rate swap is a contract which commits two counterparties to exchange, over an agreed period, two streams of interest payments, each calculated using a different interest rate index, but applied to a common notional principal amount.

An example

Take an interest rate swap which commits Bank A to pay Bank Z, over a period of *three years*, a stream of interest payments calculated using a long-term *US dollar* interest rate in exchange for Bank Z paying Bank A, over the same period, a counterstream of interest payments calculated using the six-month US dollar Libor index, both applied to a common notional principal amount of US$10m[1]. The example is illustrated in the diagram below.

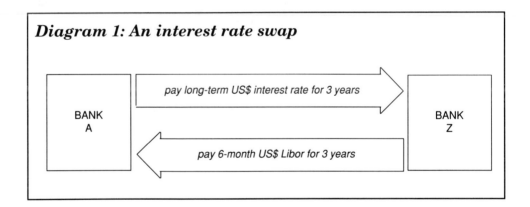

Diagram 1: An interest rate swap

BANK A — pay long-term US$ interest rate for 3 years → BANK Z

BANK Z — pay 6-month US$ Libor for 3 years → BANK A

■ The *tenor* of the long-term interest rate used to calculate the interest paid by Bank A is the same as that of the swap (ie, three years). The interest rate is therefore fixed over the life of the swap and is accordingly called a **fixed** interest rate. Because the interest rate is fixed, the stream of interest paid by Bank A will consist of *equal* or *similar* interest amounts, each calculated at the fixed rate and known, in advance, from the commencement of the swap[2]. The fixed interest rate will be in line with yields on bonds of the same tenor.

■ The six-month Libor used to calculate the interest paid by Bank Z applies to periods of six months only. Specifically, a particular six-month Libor applies to the six-month *interest period* following its fixing. However, the swap is for three years. Consequently, once a six-month interest period expires, a new rate for six-month Libor must be fixed for the next six-month interest period. Given the three-year tenor of the swap, six-month Libor is in fact fixed at the commencement of the swap and then refixed five more times: after six, 12, 18, 24 and 30 months. Where Libor has to be refixed in this way, it is called a **floating** interest rate. Because Libor is a floating rate, the stream of interest paid by Bank Z will consist of variable amounts, which will change every six months in line with Libor. Only the first floating interest amount will be known in advance, as it is fixed at the commencement of the swap.

■ As the interest rate assumes interest is paid *annually*, three **payments** might be made from Bank A to Bank Z over the three-year life of the swap (at the end of each year). If a semi-annual interest rate had been used (on which interest is paid semi-annually), there might have been six payments.

■ Given that the Libor index used in the swap has a *six-month tenor*, there would normally be six *semi-annual* payments from Bank Z to Bank A over the three-year life of the swap (at the end of each six-month period). If the index chosen had been three-month Libor, there would normally be twelve quarterly payments. The interest streams involved in the swap are illustrated in Diagram 2 below.

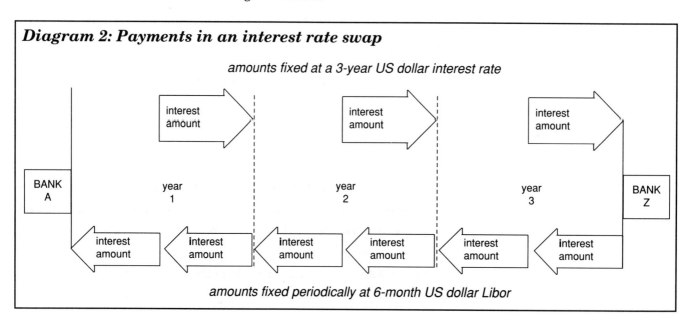

Diagram 2: Payments in an interest rate swap

amounts fixed at a 3-year US dollar interest rate

amounts fixed periodically at 6-month US dollar Libor

- Where the number of payments to be exchanged through a swap might differ because of payment conventions (as in this example), in practice, it is usual to split up the less frequent payments or combine the more frequent payments to ensure there are equal numbers. This practice allows payments to be **netted**, thereby reducing credit risk.

- Only *interest* is exchanged in the swap: there is no exchange of *principal*. Although the *size* of the swap contract is measured in terms of its **notional principal amount** (US$10m in the example above), this figure is used only to calculate the interest amounts to be exchanged. Because an interest rate swap does not therefore impact on the *balance sheets* of the swap counterparties (only on their *profit and loss accounts*), it is classed as an **off-balance sheet** instrument.

- Interest rate swaps are classed, not only as off-balance sheet instruments, but also as **derivative** financial instruments. Derivatives are a special type of off-balance sheet instrument on which no principal is ever paid. Derivatives make payments calculated using prices or interest rates 'derived' from *on-balance sheet* or **cash** instruments, but do not actually employ those cash instruments to fund the payments. The cash instruments from which the swap in the example derived its interest rates were a three-year bond and a six-month Eurodollar deposit (remember, Libor is an interest rate on Eurocurrency deposits). Some off-balance sheet instruments involve exchanges of principal and are therefore not classed as derivatives. For example, forward foreign exchange contracts are off-balance sheet, because they are future commitments which do not immediately affect the balance sheet, but they are not derivatives, because there is an *eventual* exchange of principal.

Analysing swaps

To make them easier to understand, interest rate swaps are often illustrated with simple *box-and-arrow* diagrams, as shown below. The technique is strongly recommended, particularly for those new to swaps. In this Workbook, a straight line is used to represent fixed interest streams and a wavy line to represent floating interest streams.

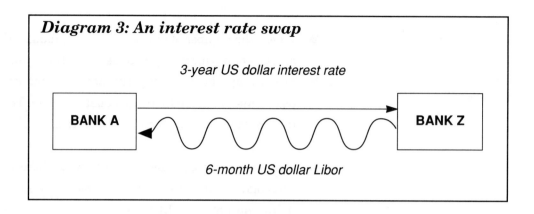

Diagram 3: An interest rate swap

3-year US dollar interest rate

BANK A

BANK Z

6-month US dollar Libor

Interest rate swaps and other types of 'swap'

There can be confusion between interest rate swaps and **currency swaps**. Currency swaps are a special type of interest rate swap in which the interest streams being swapped are denominated in different currencies. Currency swaps also involve an exchange of principal. Where the term 'interest rate swap' is used on its own, it can usually be taken to mean a *single currency* rather than a cross-currency interest rate swap.

Interest rate swaps should not be confused with **foreign exchange swaps**. There is a relationship, in that foreign exchange swaps perform a similar function to currency swaps in taking and hedging currency risk, but there are important differences in the way they do this.

The terminology of interest rate swaps

Coupon swap

The interest rate swap in the example above involved the exchange of an interest stream based on a *fixed* interest rate for an interest stream based on a *floating* interest rate (Libor). Such **fixed-against-floating** swaps are called **coupon** swaps. The term reflects the fact that the fixed interest rates used in such swaps reflect the yields on fixed-income or *coupon*-bearing bonds, which pay fixed nominal amounts of interest, often called 'coupons' (after the certificates which traditionally evidence the right of a bondholder to specific interest payments). Coupon swaps are the most commonly traded type of interest rate swap.

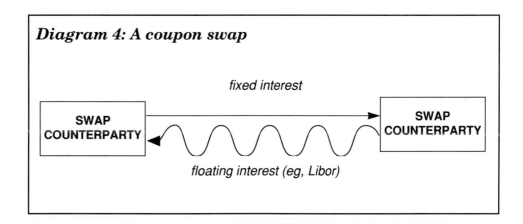

Diagram 4: A coupon swap

Generic swap

Generic is a term used to describe the simplest of any type of financial instrument (the so-called *straight* or *plain vanilla* versions). Specifically, a generic interest rate swap has:

■ a constant *notional principal amount*;

■ an exchange of *fixed-against-floating* interest: in other words, a generic swap is a simple type of *coupon swap*;

■ a constant *fixed interest* rate;

■ a flat *floating interest* rate (ie, no margin over the index);

■ regular (but not necessarily simultaneous) *payment* of fixed and floating interest;

- an immediate (or spot) *start*;

- no special *risk features* (eg, a combination with an option).

All the more complex *(non-generic)* types of interest rate swap can be constructed from the generic instrument, by combining generic swaps in complicated structures or by adding other derivatives like futures and options. This Workbook is limited to generic swaps, in order to provide a clear introduction to the subject of swaps.

It is possible to swap two interest streams which are both calculated using *floating* interest rates. These **floating-against-floating** swaps are non-generic swaps and are called **basis** (or sometimes **index**) swaps.

Basis swap

Basis swaps can involve a variety of combinations of floating interest rate indexes:

- *different tenors* of the same interest rate index, eg, three-month Libor against six-month Libor;

- the same or different tenors of *different interest rate indexes*, eg, three-month US dollar Libor against three-month US Treasury bill yield, or six-month US dollar Libor against the US Prime rate;

- the same tenor of the same interest rate index, but with one index carrying a *margin,* (a basis point is one one-hundredth of a percent, ie, 0.01%) eg, three-month Libor against three-month Libor + 50 basis points.

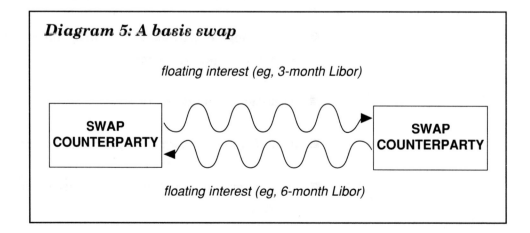

Diagram 5: A basis swap

floating interest (eg, 3-month Libor)

SWAP COUNTERPARTY

SWAP COUNTERPARTY

floating interest (eg, 6-month Libor)

There are no true **fixed-against-fixed** single-currency interest rate swaps. The technique is used, not for interest rate management, but for cash-flow management purposes. There are fixed-against-fixed cross-currency swaps (called *currency swap*s).

Asset swap

Where the interest streams being exchanged through an interest rate swap are funded with interest received on specific assets, the swap is called an **asset swap**. It is important to note that an asset swap does not involve any change in the swap mechanism itself. The term simply identifies the *purpose* of the swap. It is therefore possible to have an asset swap which is also a coupon or basis swap. An asset swap may be sold as a package with underlying assets, but the swap and the assets themselves remain otherwise separate instruments in that they can be, and usually are, contracts between different sets of counterparties.

Given the existence of the term 'asset swap', interest rate swaps not identified with specific assets, but associated with specific liabilities, should logically be called **liability swaps**. However, this term is rarely used in practice and a swap which is not an asset swap is usually just referred to as an 'interest rate swap'.

Term swap

A swap with an original tenor of more than two years is usually referred to as a **term swap**. The fixed interest rates paid through such swaps reflect the yields on fixed-income bonds of the same tenor (see *Part Four* on *Pricing and Valuing Swaps*).

Money market swap

A swap with an original tenor of up to two years is usually referred to as a **money market swap.** The fixed interest rates paid through such swaps reflect the fixed interest rates available by hedging with other short-term interest rate derivatives, particularly futures (see *Part Four* on *Pricing and Valuing Swaps*). There is a special class of money market swaps which have tenors corresponding exactly to those of continuous sequence of short-term interest rate futures contracts (see *Part Three* on *Trading Swaps*): in the US dollar market, such swaps are called **IMM swaps**, as the futures contracts are the three-month Eurodollar futures contract traded on the IMM or International Monetary Market, a division of the Chicago Mercantile Exchange (CME).

Counterparties to a coupon swap

In order to distinguish the counterparties to a coupon swap, one is termed the **payer** and the other, the **receiver**. The paying and receiving refer to the *fixed* interest stream in a coupon swap. The terms are illustrated in Diagram 6 below.

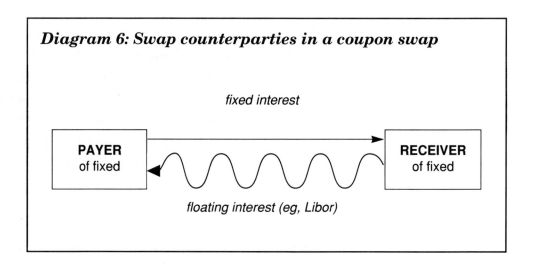

Diagram 6: Swap counterparties in a coupon swap

fixed interest

| PAYER of fixed | | RECEIVER of fixed |

floating interest (eg, Libor)

Counterparties to a basis swap

In a basis swap, the convention of calling one counterparty a payer and the other a receiver becomes ambiguous and it is good practice to describe each counterparty in terms of *both* the interest stream it pays and the interest stream it receives. See Diagram 7.

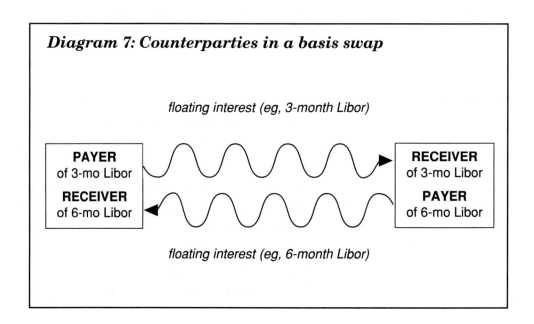

Diagram 7: Counterparties in a basis swap

floating interest (eg, 3-month Libor)

PAYER of 3-mo Libor
RECEIVER of 6-mo Libor

RECEIVER of 3-mo Libor
PAYER of 6-mo Libor

floating interest (eg, 6-month Libor)

Alternative terms for swap counterparties

Sometimes, the terms **buyer** and **seller** are used to describe swap counterparties. These terms are not intuitively obvious and usage in the market can be contradictory. Their use is therefore discouraged when transacting in the swap market. In coupon swaps, the terms refer to the *obligation to pay fixed interest*. Thus, a swap *buyer pays the fixed* and receives the floating interest stream. A swap *seller receives the fixed* and pays the floating interest stream. See Diagram 8 below.

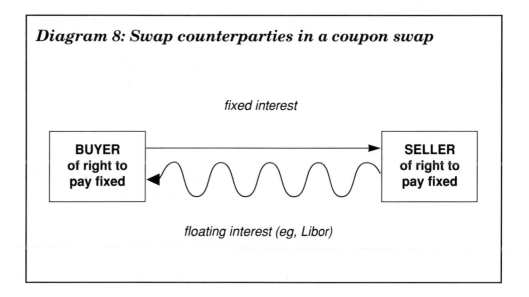

Diagram 8: Swap counterparties in a coupon swap

How swap prices are quoted	It has become a convention in the swap market to use Libor as the standard index for the floating interest rate in coupon swaps in most currencies (usually *six-month* Libor). Other floating-rate indexes are available, but the presumption in most swap markets is that the floating-rate index is Libor, unless otherwise specified[3]. It is therefore possible to discuss the 'price' of coupon swaps solely in terms of their *fixed* rates and the swap market is sometimes said to 'talk the fixed [rate]'. The fixed interest rate in a coupon swap is called the **swap rate**.

All-in prices	In the early days of the interest rate swap market, and still in the case of currencies which have less liquid swap markets, the fixed rates in coupon swaps are quoted in *absolute* terms, ie, as the full percentage annual yield. These so-called **all-in** prices are illustrated in the reproduction below of the table of New Zealand dollar swap prices which is published each week in *International Financing Review*.

Table 1: Example of 'all-in' swap rates

New Zealand dollar swaps

Year	Semi-annual rate
1 year	8.00–7.85
2 years	8.25–8.05
3 years	8.50–8.30
4 years	8.85–8.65
5 years	9.05–8.85
7 years	9.25–9.05

Source: International Financing Review, Bankers Trust New Zealand Ltd

Two-way prices	In Table 1 above, it can be seen that two prices are quoted for each maturity of interest rate swap. These are **two-way** prices. A 'two-way' price is typically quoted between professional swap dealers and is a dual quotation consisting of a *buying* and a *selling* price for each instrument. However, as explained already, the terms 'buying' and 'selling' can be ambiguous in the

case of swaps, so they are usually substituted by the terms 'paying' and 'receiving'. Which of the two quoted prices is being paid and which is being received may not seem obvious. However, it only needs to be remembered that the dealer quoting the prices will be aiming to make a profit, if swaps can be transacted at both prices. This means paying the *lower* fixed rate in one swap and receiving the *higher* fixed rate in the other, thereby earning the **dealing spread** between the two rates. For example, in the case of seven-year New Zealand dollar swaps quoted in Table 1 above, the quoting dealer will hope to receive a fixed rate of 9.25% per annum and pay a fixed rate of 9.05%, earning a spread of 20 basis points per annum on every matching pair of swaps. The objective which underlies two-way price quotes is illustrated in the diagram below for the example given above.

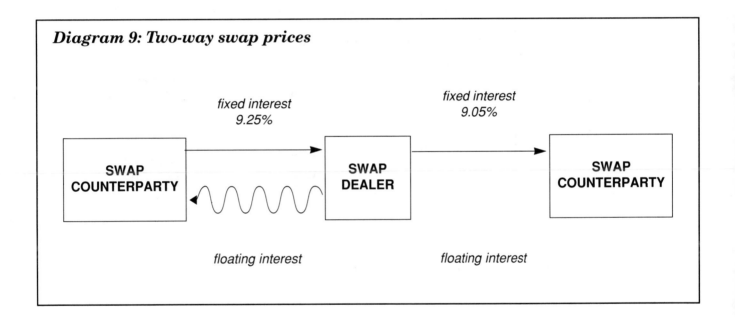

Diagram 9: Two-way swap prices

Swap spreads

In swap markets in certain major currencies, such as US dollars, the use of all-in terms for quoting the fixed rates in coupon swaps has been replaced by the convention of quoting in two parts: a **swap spread** and a **benchmark** interest rate. The benchmark interest rate is usually the yield on the **on-the-run** (most liquid) government bond with a remaining maturity closest to that of the swap. When a coupon swap is agreed, the spread and benchmark yield are fixed, producing an all-in rate which is used in calculating the fixed-interest payments through the swap. Swap spreads therefore, are quoted while negotiating a swap, before it is agreed and implemented. The convention of quoting swap prices in terms of spreads over a benchmark bond yield is illustrated in the reproduction below of the table of US dollar coupon swap prices published each week in *International Financing Review* (this table also gives the equivalent all-in swap rates). The use of swap spreads is a convention adopted from the debt capital market. The convention has been adopted for swaps because the fixed interest rates used in swaps reflect bond yields and many swaps are undertaken as complementary transactions to new bond issues (see *Part Two* on *Using Swaps*), making it convenient to price swaps in terms comparable to the bonds with which they are to be used.

Table 2: Example of swap spreads

Interest rate swap quotations

US dollars	Spread	Annual interest A/360
2 years	21/25	5.70–5.75
3 years	40/45	6.23–6.28
5 years	46/51	7.01–7.05
7 years	46/51	7.46–7.51
10 years	47/52	7.93–7.97

Source: International Financing Review, Euro Brokers Ltd

The prices quoted in Table 2 are two-way prices. For example, the current price of a five-year US dollar coupon swap is quoted as a two-way swap spread of '46/51'. The lower price of '46' means the dealer giving the quote is willing to transact swaps in which he pays a fixed rate of 46 basis points over the yield on the most liquid five-year US Treasury note. The higher price of '51' means the dealer giving the quote is also willing to transact swaps in which he receives a fixed rate of 51 basis points over the yield on the most liquid five-year US Treasury note. The equivalent *all-in* rates at the time the table was compiled were 7.01% and 7.05% per annum[4].

What does an interest rate swap do?

Interest rate swaps and interest rate risk

Each counterparty in an interest rate swap is committed to pay the other counterparty a stream of interest, in exchange for receiving a different stream of interest. The two interest streams being swapped differ in terms of being calculated using different interest rate indexes. Different indexes are likely to behave differently over time. Therefore, each counterparty to a swap is exposed to the risk that, during the life of the swap, the differential between the two indexes will change such that the floating interest paid through the swap will increase or the floating interest received will decrease or (in the case of basis swaps) both, the *net* effect of which will be to reduce the overall profitability of the swap, or create or increase a loss. In other words, an interest rate swap creates an exposure to *interest rate risk*.

Interest rate risk created by coupon swaps

Take the three-year US dollar coupon swap used in the earlier example. This is illustrated in Diagram 10. The long-term interest rate paid by Bank A through the swap is fixed, so that its interest payments to Bank Z do not change over the life of the swap. However, the six-month Libor paid by Bank Z through the swap is a floating rate, so its payments to Bank A periodically change, in line with market fluctuations in Libor. The net effect on the profitability of the swap therefore depends on how six-month Libor changes relative to the fixed long-term interest rate. Bank A (the payer of fixed and receiver of floating interest) makes a loss when six-month Libor falls below the three-year interest rate over Libor refixing date. Bank Z (the receiver of fixed and payer of floating interest) starts to move into loss when six-month Libor rises above the three-year interest rate. The risk created by the coupon swap is illustrated in Diagram 10 on the following page.

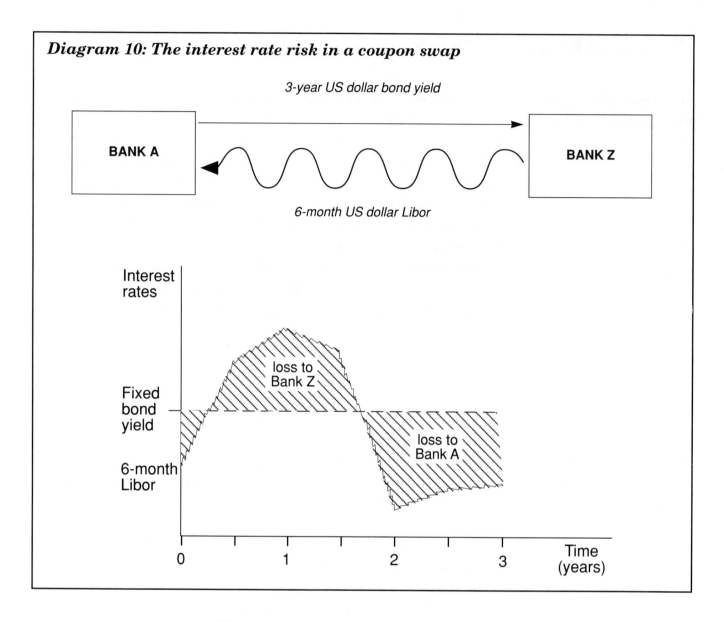

Diagram 10: The interest rate risk in a coupon swap

There are a number of points about the interest rate risk in coupon swaps to note from the example:

■ The six-month Libor index used in the swap is normally updated every six months, while the three-year interest rate remains fixed at the level agreed when the swap was transacted. Therefore, the floating interest stream will tend to reflect *current* interest rate levels, while the fixed interest stream will reflect an *historic* level. In other words, the profitability of a coupon swap broadly reflects the general trend in interest rates after the commencement of the swap. The interest rate risk created by a coupon swap is therefore essentially one of an *absolute* change in interest rates.

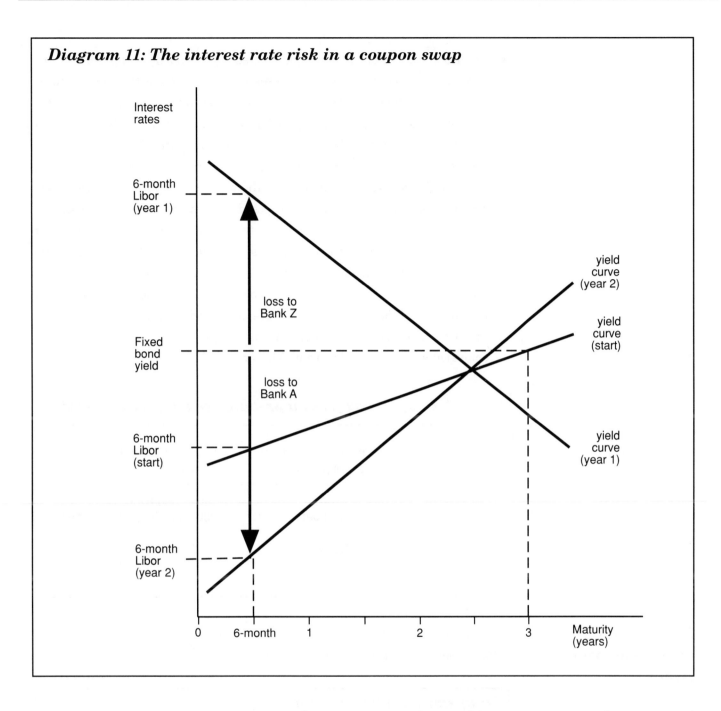

Diagram 11: The interest rate risk in a coupon swap

- Because the interest rate risk created by a coupon swap reflects its use of interest rate indexes of different tenors (six months and three years in the example), the risk is one of a change in the slope of the *yield curve* across its six-month to three-year sector. Interest rate swaps therefore help to integrate the money and capital markets. This aspect of interest rate risk is illustrated in Diagram 11 above, which charts the profitability of a coupon swap as the yield curve rotates.

■ As noted, the interest rate risk created by a coupon swap reflects the difference in the tenors of the indexes used to calculate the interest to be exchanged in the swap. The same risk is created when a maturity mismatch or **gap** is opened by borrowing and lending cash instruments of different tenors. A coupon swap, therefore, performs an equivalent function *off balance sheet* to that performed *on balance sheet* by 'gapping'. This can be seen from the swap in the example. Bank A, as the payer of the three-year bond yield and receiver of six-month Libor, is exposed to the same interest rate risk as if it had borrowed through issuance of a three-year bond (paying a three-year bond yield) and lent through placing six-month Eurodeposits (earning six-month Libor). Bank Z, on the other hand, as the receiver of fixed and payer of floating interest, is exposed to the same risk as if it had borrowed for six months by taking six-month Eurodeposits and lent for three years by investing in a three-year bond. Coupon swaps and their on-balance sheet equivalents are compared in Table 3 below.

Table 3: Coupon swaps and on-balance sheet equivalents

	Off-balance sheet (ie, coupon swap)	**On-balance sheet** (ie, gapping)
Bank A	pay fixed receive floating	issue bond/pay fixed place deposit/receive floating
Bank Z	pay floating receive fixed	take deposit/pay floating buy bond/receive fixed

Interest rate risk created by basis swaps

Take the example of a basis swap between three-month and six-month US dollar Libor as illustrated in Diagram 12.

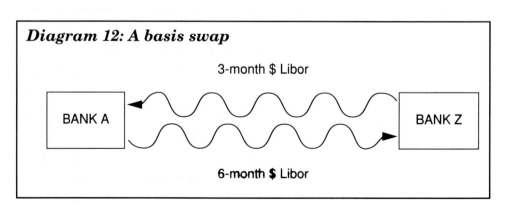

Diagram 12: A basis swap

3-month $ Libor

BANK A ⟵⟶ BANK Z

6-month **$** Libor

Diagram 13 below shows the past performance of three-month and six-month US dollar Libor, and the *basis* between them (six-month Libor minus three-month Libor). Where six-month Libor exceeded three-month Libor and the differential was positive on Libor refixing dates (eg, 1987–88), the basis swap in the example would have made a profit for Bank Z. Where three-month Libor exceeds six-month Libor and the differential was negative on Libor refixing dates (eg, 1990–92), the swap would have made a profit for Bank A.

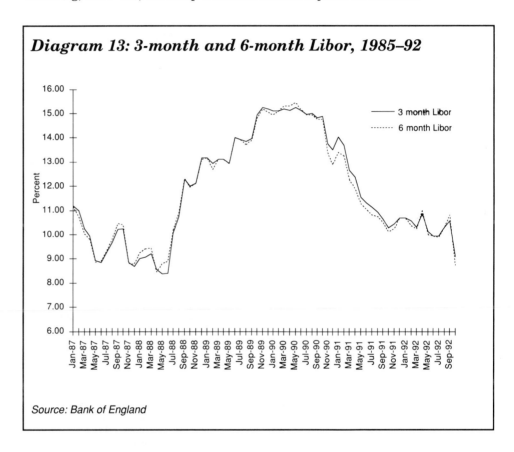

Diagram 13: 3-month and 6-month Libor, 1985–92

Source: Bank of England

There are a number of points about the interest rate risk in basis swaps to note from this example:

■ The performance of a basis swap depends upon the *relative* change in the two floating interest rate indexes (whereas coupon swaps reflect the absolute changes in floating interest rates). Changes in the absolute levels of three-month and six-month Libor have no impact on the profitability of a basis swap, unless the two indexes increase or decrease by different amounts and thereby change the *differential* between them. The interest rate risk exposure which a basis swap creates is called **basis risk**.

■ Basis swaps can, like coupon swaps, provide an off-balance sheet equivalent to on-balance sheet gapping. However, floating interest rate indexes have *short-term* tenors (typically, no more than six months) and so basis swaps therefore only allow gapping across the limited segment of the short-term yield curve covered by the money market.

Notes

1. The frequency of fixed interest payments follows the convention in the bond market in the relevant currency. Thus, sterling and US dollar swaps tend to pay semi-annual fixed interest.

2. Whether the fixed interest amounts are equal or not depends on how annual interest rates are divided into sub-annual periods (eg, semi-annual or quarterly). In some markets, annual interest rates are equally divided, whereas other markets divide by the ratio of the day count to the annual basis, which may change slightly between periods.

3. While **term swaps** tend to use six-month Libor as the floating-interest rate index, **money market swaps** also often use three-month Libor and other three-month indexes. The fixed interest rate used in **term swaps** tends to follow the convention in the bond market in the relevant currency. Thus, sterling and US dollar swaps tend to pay **semi-annual** fixed interest. The fixed interest rate used in **money market swaps** can be quarterly, semi-annual or annual. The combinations of fixed and floating interest rates in money market swaps are usually:

quarterly fixed/quarterly floating (called *quarterly-quarterly*)
semi-annual fixed/semi-annual floating (called *semi-semi*)
annual fixed/quarterly floating (called *annual-threes*)

4. All-in rates of 7.01–7.05% are quoted on an annual basis, whereas US Treasury yields (and spreads) are quoted semi-annually. The all-in rates on a semi-annual basis are 6.89% and 6.93%, respectively. With the swap spreads of 46/51, this implies that US Treasury note yields were 6.43% (= 7.01–0.46) and 6.42% (= 6.93–0.51). It may seem odd that the left-hand number of a two-way price quotation (the buying quote) is larger than the right-hand number (the selling quote). The fact that the benchmark Treasury notes are quoted as '6.43%–6.42%' is, however, not a mistake. The Treasury notes are quoted in the market in *price* rather than yield terms. Therefore, in a given two-way quote, the quote to buy them (the 'bid') should be lower than the related quote to sell them (the 'offer') only when a *price* is being quoted. Given the inverse relationship between the price and yield for fixed-income securities like US Treasury notes, converting the prices of Treasury notes into *yield* terms will produce quotations which appear to be in reverse order.

Self-Study Exercises: <u>Questions</u>   Part 1

Question 1.1:   Fill in the blank spaces in the following definition of an interest rate swap:

An interest rate swap is a contract which commits two counterparties to _____, over an agreed period, two _____, each calculated using a different _____, but applied to a common _____.

Question 1.2:   Assume a five-year US dollar coupon swap involving three-month Libor. How many floating interest payments would there usually be in this swap?

Question 1.3:   Identify which of the following interest rate swaps are coupon, basis, asset or currency swaps:

    3.1   between three-month US dollar Libor and six-month US dollar Libor?

    3.2   between three-month US dollar Libor and the interest from a five-year Eurobond?

    3.3   between three-month US dollar Libor and a five-year US dollar bond yield?

    3.4   between three-month US dollar Libor and six-month sterling Libor?

    3.5   between three-month US dollar Libor and US Prime Rate?

Question 1.4:   In the interest rate swap illustrated below, who is the *payer* and who is the *receiver*?

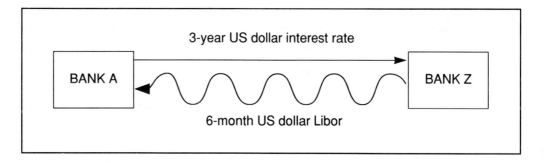

Question 1.5:   In the interest rate swap illustrated in Question 1.4 above, who is the *buyer* and who is the *seller*?

Interest rate swaps

Question 1.6: In the interest rate swap illustrated below, who is the *payer* and who is the *receiver*?

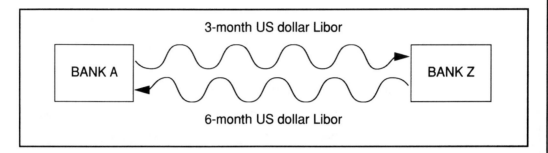

Question 1.7: Using the reference table at the end of this section, determine the price of the interest rate swap in Question 1.4, if Bank A makes the quote?

Question 1.8: Using the reference table at the end of this section, fill in the prices quoted by the bank to each of its counterparties in the interest rate swaps illustrated below.

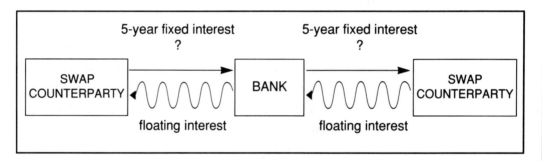

Question 1.9: In the interest rate swap illustrated in Question 1.4 above, which counterparty would gain and which would lose, if the relevant section of the yield curve *rotated anticlockwise* and *steepened*?

Question 1.10: What is the *on-balance sheet* equivalent for Bank Z of the coupon swap in Question 1.4 above? In other words, with what sort of *cash* instruments could Bank Z replicate the coupon swap in Question 1.4?

US dollars	Spread	Annual interest A/360
2 years	21/25	5.70—5.75
3 years	40/45	6.23—6.28
5 years	46/51	7.01—7.05
7 years	46/51	7.46—7.51
10 years	47/52	7.93—7.97

Self-Study Exercises: <u>Answers</u> **Part 1**

Answer 1.1: The complete definition of an interest rate swap is:

An interest rate swap is a contract which commits two counterparties to *exchange*, over an agreed period, two *streams of interest payments*, each calculated using a different *interest rate index*, but applied to a common *notional principal amount*.

Answer 1.2: There would usually be *20 quarterly* floating interest payments over the life of the swap or four each year, reflecting the quarterly tenor of the floating rate index.

Answer 1.3:
3.1   This floating-against-floating US dollar swap is a *basis* swap.

3.2   This fixed-against-floating US dollar swap is a *coupon* swap, but as the fixed payments in the swap are funded from a specific asset, it is also an *asset* swap.

3.3   This fixed-against-floating US dollar swap is a *coupon* swap.

3.4   This floating-against-floating swap is a *basis* swap, but the two indexes are denominated in different currencies, so it is also a *currency* swap.

3.5   This floating-against-floating US dollar swap is a *basis* swap.

Answer 1.4: The 'payer' in this swap is Bank A and the 'receiver' is Bank Z, as the terms refer to the payment and receipt of the fixed interest stream.

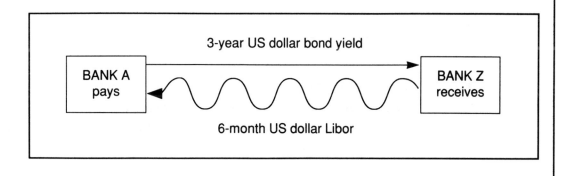

Answer 1.5: The 'buyer' in this swap is Bank A and the 'seller' is Bank Z, as the terms refer to the buying and selling of the obligation to pay the fixed interest stream.

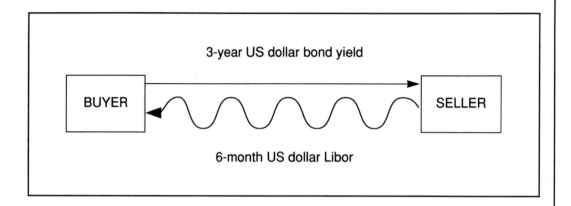

Answer 1.6: *Both* counterparties are referred to as 'payers' and 'receivers' in a basis swap such as the one in Question 1.6, as there is no generally-accepted convention for distinguishing between floating interest rate indexes. It is good practice to identify each swap counterparty in terms of both the floating interest stream it pays and the floating interest stream it receives.

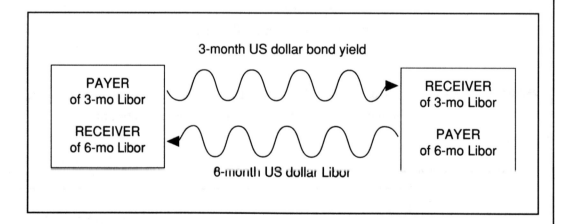

Answer 1.7: The two-way price for a three-year swap quoted in the reference table is 6.23–6.28%. As Bank A is quoting the price and is paying the fixed interest rate, it will want to pay the lower interest rate and will therefore quote the lower side of the two-way price. This is **6.23%**.

Answer 1.8: The prices quoted by the bank to each of its counterparties are set out below in the diagram. The bank quotes with the aim of paying the lower and receiving the higher fixed interest rate. The price quotations can be in terms of 'all-in' prices or 'swap spreads over a benchmark yield' (which will be the yield on five-year US Treasury notes in this case).

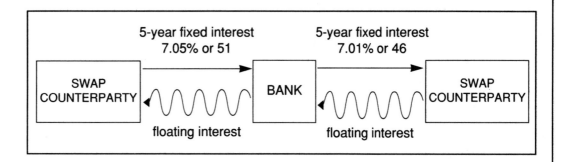

Answer 1.9: Bank Z will gain. The anticlockwise rotation and steepening of the yield curve across its six-month to three-year section will lower the six-month end of the yield curve and raise the three-year end. This movement will reduce the six-month floating interest payments which Bank Z is committed to make to Bank A through the swap. The three-year fixed interest payments which Bank A is committed to pay Bank Z through the swap will, of course, not change.

Answer 1.10: In the swap in Question 1.4, Bank Z is the *receiver* of fixed interest at a three-year US dollar bond yield and the payer of floating interest at six-month US dollar Libor. The on-balance sheet equivalent would be for Bank Z to receive the coupons on a three-year US dollar bond and pay the interest on a six-month Eurodollar deposit. In other words, to replicate the coupon swap, Bank Z should *invest* in a three-year US dollar bond and *fund* that investment with six-month Eurodollar deposits.

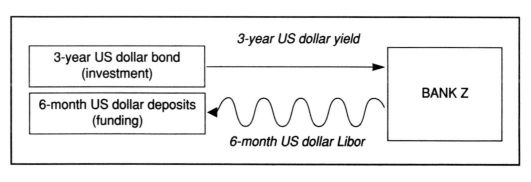

2 Using swaps

Risk management with swaps: taking risk

In *Part One*, it was explained that an interest rate swap creates an exposure to the risk of a change in interest rates. Interest rate swaps can therefore be used to take *risk positions* based upon expectations about the direction in which interest rates will move in the future.

Using interest rate swaps to take independent interest rate risk

Interest rate swaps can be used to take risk positions *independent* of any underlying instruments. The types of interest rate risk created by transacting swaps was discussed in *Part One*. Thus:

- the *payer* of fixed interest in a coupon swap is exposed to the risk of an interest rate *fall*;

- the *receiver* of fixed interest in a coupon swap is exposed to the risk of an interest rate *rise*.

Using interest rate swaps to manage interest rate risk with other instruments

In practice, interest rate swaps are usually used to manage risk positions in *conjunction* with cash instruments. Swaps can be used to manage interest rate risk on:

- individual instruments;

- balance sheets.

Using swaps with individual instruments

In a situation where there is an existing exposure to interest rate risk, interest rate swaps can be used to change that risk. Take an example in which a company has issued a fixed-income bond. The company is exposed to the risk of a fall in interest rates, which will leave it paying a higher rate of interest on its borrowing than necessary. If the company expects and wishes to benefit from a fall in interest rates, it needs to exchange its fixed-interest obligation for a floating-interest obligation before rates fall. It would be difficult, if not impossible, for the company to achieve this switch on its balance sheet by substituting its fixed-income bond with a new floating-rate liability. However, the company could more readily achieve the same effect with an interest rate swap. This is illustrated in Diagram 14.

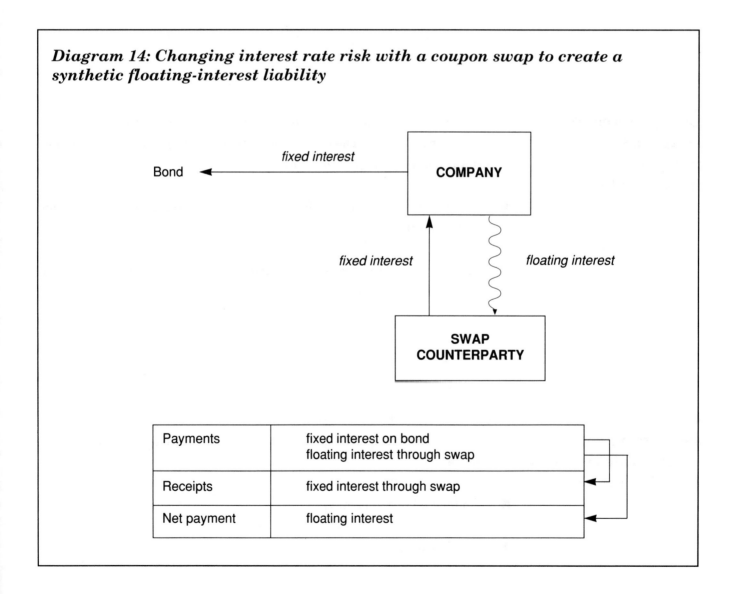

Diagram 14: Changing interest rate risk with a coupon swap to create a synthetic floating-interest liability

By putting on a coupon swap in which it receives fixed and pays floating interest, the company can effectively convert its fixed-income bond to a floating-rate liability. The fixed interest received through the swap would be used to fund and offset the fixed-interest payments on the bond, leaving the company paying floating interest through the swap. The company would still have the fixed-income bond on its balance sheet, but the swap would have changed the cash flow characteristics of this liability. The coupon swap can be said to have created a **synthetic** floating-rate liability.

Coupon swaps can also be used to synthesise fixed-interest liabilities from floating-interest liabilities, as illustrated in Diagram 15.

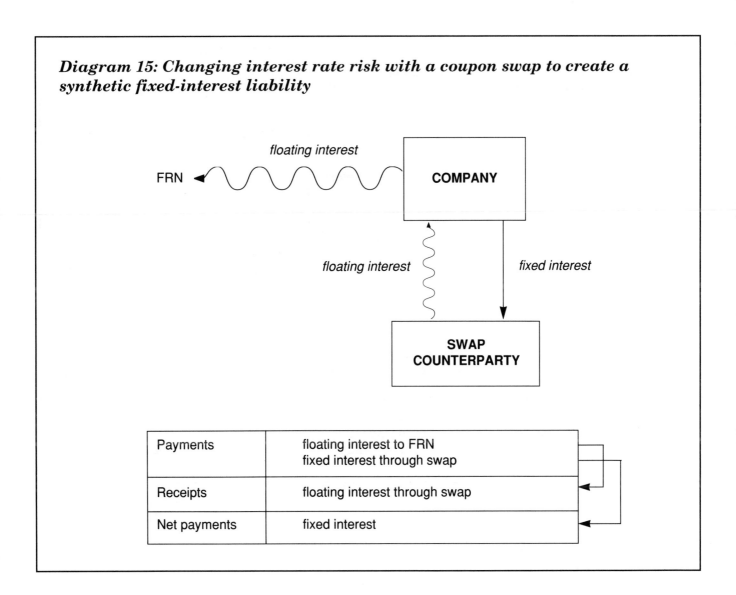

Diagram 15: Changing interest rate risk with a coupon swap to create a synthetic fixed-interest liability

Payments	floating interest to FRN fixed interest through swap
Receipts	floating interest through swap
Net payments	fixed interest

Another alternative, the synthesis of fixed-interest assets from floating-interest assets, is illustrated in Diagram 16 below.

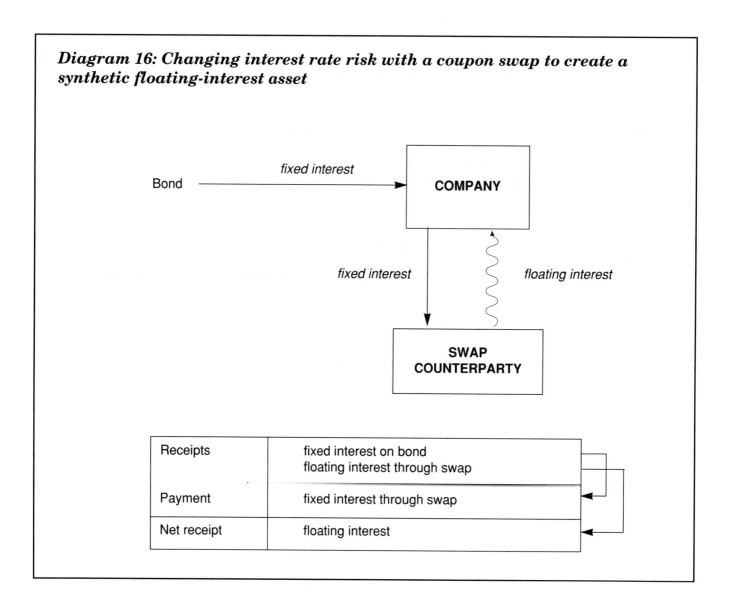

Diagram 16: Changing interest rate risk with a coupon swap to create a synthetic floating-interest asset

Receipts	fixed interest on bond floating interest through swap
Payment	fixed interest through swap
Net receipt	floating interest

Finally, coupon swaps can be used to synthesise fixed-interest assets from floating-interest assets, as illustrated in Diagram 17 below.

Diagram 17: Changing interest rate risk with a coupon swap to create a synthetic fixed-interest asset

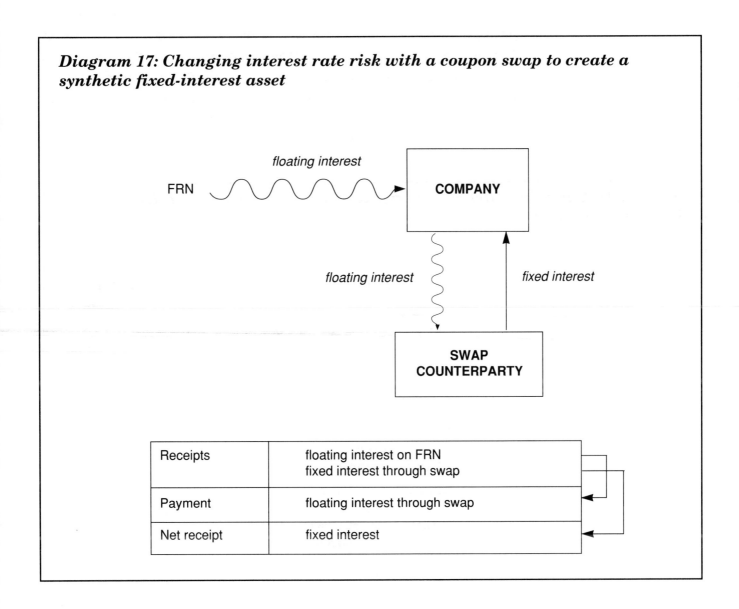

Using swaps with balance sheets

Where a risk position is the product of a mismatch between the interest rate bases of assets and liabilities on a balance sheet, it is necessary to take account of both sides. Swaps can no longer be identified simply as 'asset' or 'liability' swaps, as they are connected with both sides of the balance sheet.

An example

Take a bank with assets and liabilities which are both floating rate, meaning it has no exposure to interest rate risk[1]. If the bank expected interest rates to *rise* and wished to take a risk position based on this expectation, it could do so by putting on a coupon swap in which it is the *payer* of fixed and receiver of floating interest, as illustrated in Diagram 18 below. The floating interest received through the swap would fund and offset the floating interest paid out by the bank on its liabilities. The bank is left receiving floating interest on its assets (which will increase, if rates do rise), but paying out fixed interest through the swap (which will not change).

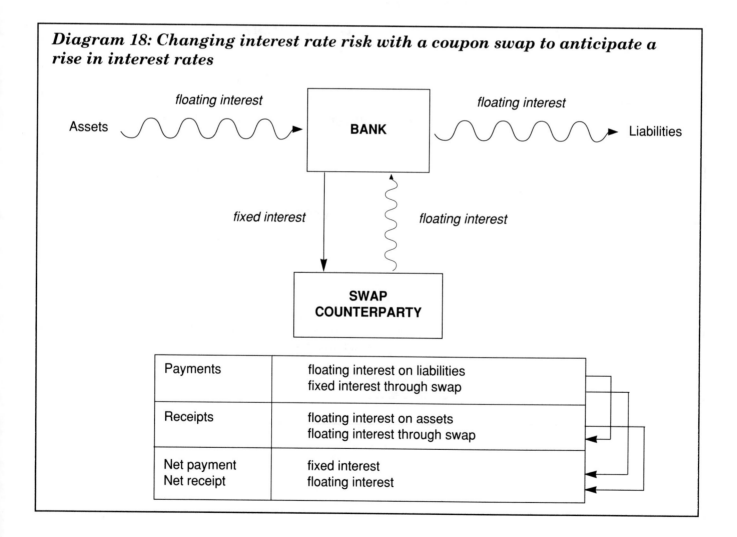

Diagram 18: Changing interest rate risk with a coupon swap to anticipate a rise in interest rates

Payments	floating interest on liabilities fixed interest through swap
Receipts	floating interest on assets floating interest through swap
Net payment Net receipt	fixed interest floating interest

If the bank in the example expected a *fall* in interest rates, it should put on a coupon swap in which it *receives* fixed interest, as illustrated in Diagram 19 below.

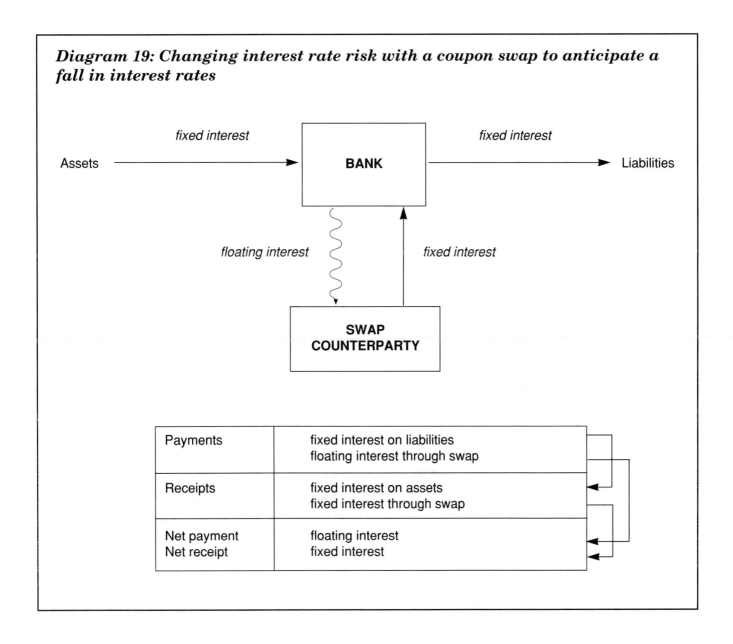

Diagram 19: Changing interest rate risk with a coupon swap to anticipate a fall in interest rates

Assets → *fixed interest* → **BANK** → *fixed interest* → Liabilities

floating interest ↕ *fixed interest*

SWAP COUNTERPARTY

Payments	fixed interest on liabilities floating interest through swap
Receipts	fixed interest on assets fixed interest through swap
Net payment Net receipt	floating interest fixed interest

Risk management with swaps: hedging risk

Definition	**A hedge is a risk taken to offset an equal and opposite risk.**

Given that an interest rate swap creates an exposure to interest rate risk, it can be used to hedge another interest rate risk by providing the necessary offsetting risk.

An example

Assume a bank has invested in assets which pay it fixed rates of interest (eg, bonds) and has funded these investments by issuing liabilities on which it pays floating rates of interest (eg, FRNs). The bank is exposed to the risk that interest rates may *rise*, increasing the cost of its funding, without the offsetting benefit of any increase in the returns on its assets.

Hedging with coupon swaps

In order to hedge its interest rate risk, the bank can use a coupon swap to take an equal and opposite exposure. The appropriate swap in the example would be one in which the bank is the *payer* of fixed and receiver of floating interest. The bank can fund fixed-interest payments through the swap with the fixed-interest returns on its assets, while it can employ the floating-interest receipts through the swap to fund the floating-interest payments on its liabilities. In other words, cash flows to and from the swap offset, respectively, cash flows from and to the bank's balance sheet, thereby hedging the interest rate risk in the latter. Any changes in current market interest rates will change payments on the bank's floating-rate liabilities, but will be offset by changes in the floating-rate receipts through the swap. The hedge is illustrated in Diagram 20.

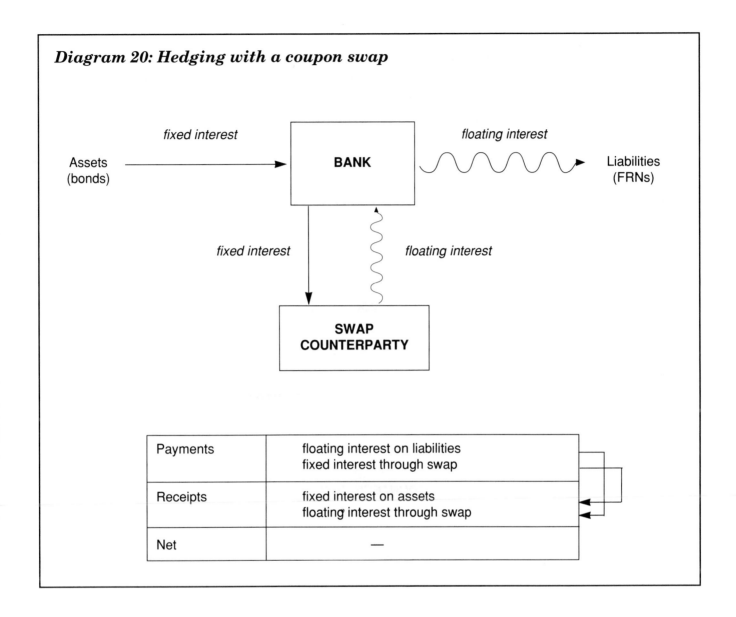

Diagram 20: Hedging with a coupon swap

The hedge illustrated above is typical of the way building societies and other mortgage lenders in the UK have been able to fund fixed-rate mortgages from floating-rate deposits, while avoiding exposure to interest rate risk.

If the bank in the example above had floating-rate assets and fixed-rate liabilities, it would have had to hedge these by putting on a coupon swap in which it was the *receiver* of the fixed interest rate, rather than the payer. This hedge is illustrated in Diagram 21 below.

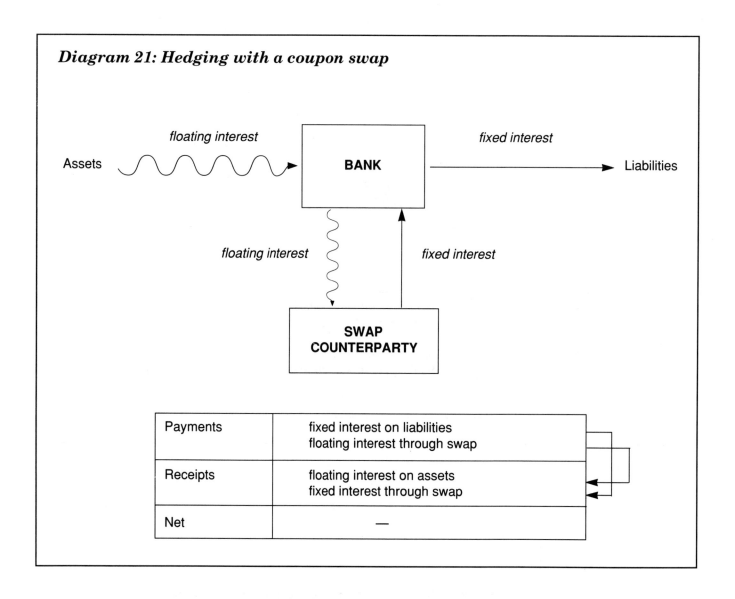

Diagram 21: Hedging with a coupon swap

The hedge illustrated above is typical of the way building societies in the UK have funded floating-rate mortgages from fixed-rate liabilities such as bonds and longer-term certificates of deposit. The same technique has been used to offer fixed-rate savings accounts to retail depositors by hedging these liabilities against floating-rate mortgage assets.

Hedging with basis swaps

Basis swaps are used to hedge mismatches between floating interest rates. Such mismatches are often between coupon swaps and basis swaps are generally used to 'tidy up' residual interest rate risks.

An example

A bank transacts two US dollar coupon swaps for different customers. The fixed interest rate in both is the same, a three-year interest rate. However, the floating-rate index in one of these swaps is three-month Libor, but six-month Libor in the other. The bank is therefore left with a basis risk between three-month and six-month Libor. The bank can hedge this risk with a basis swap between the two indexes, as illustrated in Diagram 22 below.

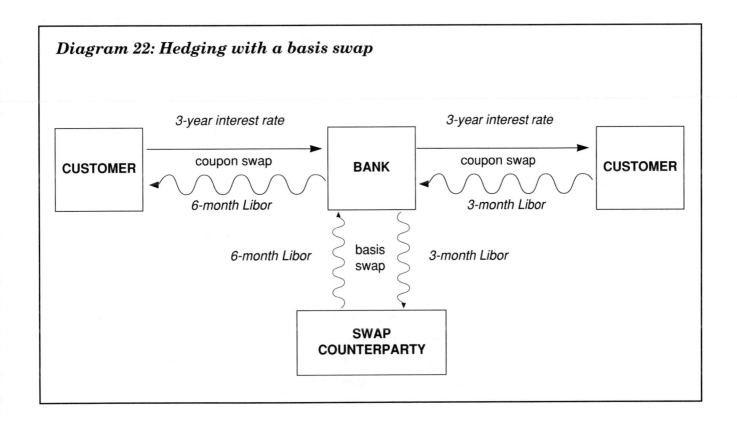

Diagram 22: Hedging with a basis swap

Return management with swaps: arbitrage with cash instruments

Definition	An arbitrage is a simultaneous sale and purchase of the same commodity at different prices to realise a profit.

In an arbitrage between an interest rate swap and a cash instrument, although different instruments are bought and sold, they will be the same 'commodity' in the sense that they both generate interest calculated using the same interest rate index. If one instrument generates a higher rate of interest than another, but they both calculate interest using the same index, then arbitrage is possible. A swap can be used to receive (or pay) interest calculated on the basis of a particular index, against a payment (or receipt) on a cash instrument of interest calculated on the basis of the same index. In an efficient market, in which the cash and derivatives markets have access to the same price information, the two rates should be the same. In practice, price discrepancies occur and give rise to arbitrage opportunities.

Arbitraging liabilities

If a swap counterparty has access to funding which is cheap relative to prevailing market rates, it can lock in this cost advantage and make a turn by putting on a swap in which it receives market interest through the swap. In effect, it is arbitraging between a cheap cash funding instrument and an expensive swap. The turn that the counterparty makes between cheap cash and expensive swap rates is used to subsidise the floating rate paid out through the swap. This type of arbitrage is illustrated below in Diagram 23. In this example, the counterparty makes a turn of 50 basis points, which means the net cost of funding is Libor minus 50bp per annum[2].

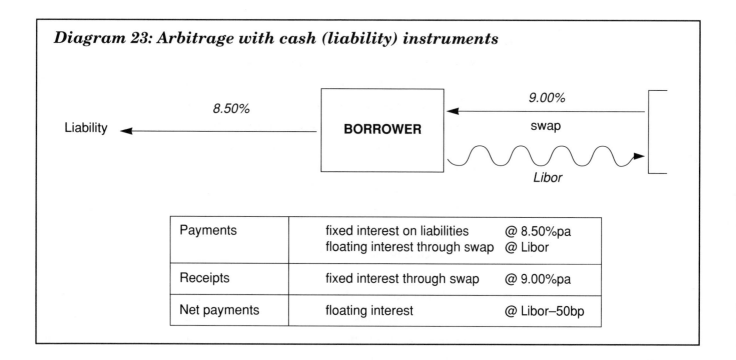

Diagram 23: Arbitrage with cash (liability) instruments

8.50%

9.00%

Liability

BORROWER

swap

Libor

Payments	fixed interest on liabilities	@ 8.50%pa
	floating interest through swap	@ Libor
Receipts	fixed interest through swap	@ 9.00%pa
Net payments	floating interest	@ Libor–50bp

Arbitrage opportunities

The differences between the cost of funding and swap rates which provide arbitrage opportunities may occur for a number of reasons:

■ Arbitrage opportunities often arise because swap rates reflect standard market yields on prime corporate bonds and therefore incorporate a premium to compensate investors for the credit risk on corporates. Swap rates are not adjusted to take account of variations in the creditworthiness of swap counterparties. Counterparties with superior credit (paying lower credit risk premia on their borrowing) are therefore likely to have access to funding at interest rates lower than those available through swaps. A common example of this **credit risk arbitrage** is between US commercial paper (USCP) and swaps in which the floating-rate index is the Federal Reserve Bank of New York's weekly USCP index for paper rated A1 by Standard & Poor's Corporation or P1 by Moody's Investors Service, the so-called *H-15 index*. Some counterparties can issue USCP at better rates than the H-15 index, which is an average, allowing them to make a turn by putting on a swap in which they receive floating interest at the H-15 rate.

■ A common source of cheap funding which provides swap arbitrage opportunities is *subsidised* finance such as export credit. Swaps are used to lock in the subsidy when interest rates are expected to fall and so reduce its value.

■ Arbitrage opportunities can arise because of variations in the *speed* at which different financial markets respond to the same information. For example, US Treasury securities react rapidly to news, whereas the US dollar bond market is somewhat slower. A retreat in the price of US Treasuries will therefore tend to force yields and swap rates (which are priced as spreads over Treasury yields) in advance of a similar response in bond yields. This opens up the possibility that bond issues can be issued cheaply enough relative to the swap rates to allow arbitrage (refer back to Diagram 23). Eventual realignment will, in part, reflect the upward pressure on bond yields exerted by new issues launched to take advantage of arbitrage opportunities.

■ *Imbalances* between the supply of and demand for securities also generate swap arbitrage opportunities. Swaps provide a method of drawing on supplies of fixed-income bonds to meet demand for floating-rate instruments by providing synthetic substitutes, or vice versa. Imbalances between supply and demand are reflected in price anomalies which create the arbitrage opportunities. For example, lack of supply and strong demand in the FRN market in 1986 sharply narrowed margins which FRNs paid over Libor. This encouraged the swapping of fixed-income bonds into synthetic FRNs, with significantly wider margins than were available on real FRNs.

Arbitraging assets

Just as interest rate swaps can be used to arbitrage cash liabilities and reduce the cost of funding, so it is also possible to use swaps to arbitrage cash assets and enhance the return on investments. An interest rate swap applied to an asset, as explained in *Part One*, is classified as an *asset swap*.

Some investors use swaps to arbitrage floating-rate assets such as FRNs, certificates of deposits and commercial paper. These assets yield above Libor, whereas the floating-rate index in swaps is normally flat Libor. The turn which can be realised between the floating interest received on the asset and the floating interest paid through the swap is used to supplement the fixed interest received through the swap, thereby creating a *synthetic* fixed-rate asset with an enhanced yield. This arbitrage is illustrated in Diagram 24.

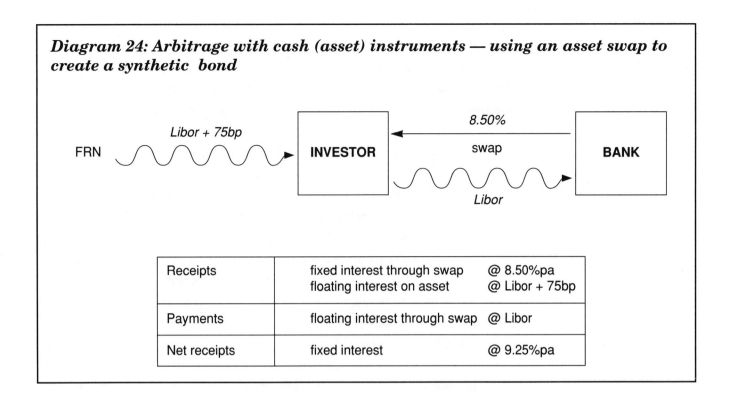

Diagram 24: Arbitrage with cash (asset) instruments — using an asset swap to create a synthetic bond

Receipts	fixed interest through swap	@ 8.50%pa
	floating interest on asset	@ Libor + 75bp
Payments	floating interest through swap	@ Libor
Net receipts	fixed interest	@ 9.25%pa

The most common use of asset swaps is to create *synthetic FRNs* from fixed-income bonds. This arbitrage is illustrated in Diagram 25.

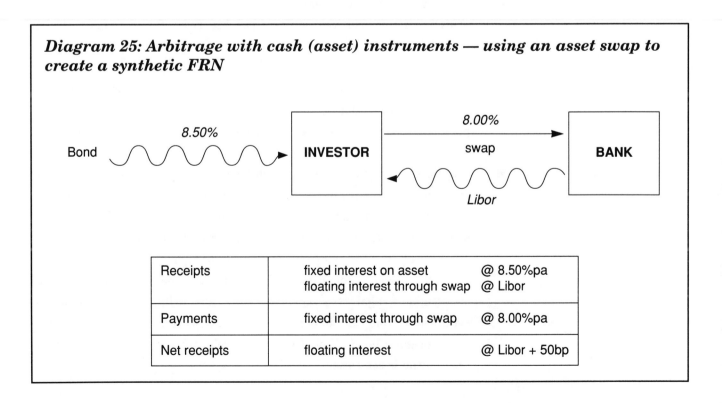

Diagram 25: Arbitrage with cash (asset) instruments — using an asset swap to create a synthetic FRN

Receipts	fixed interest on asset	@ 8.50%pa
	floating interest through swap	@ Libor
Payments	fixed interest through swap	@ 8.00%pa
Net receipts	floating interest	@ Libor + 50bp

Arbitrage opportunities

The differences between the returns on assets and swap rates which provide arbitrage opportunities usually occur where assets are especially illiquid or difficult to price. Such assets have to pay abnormally higher yields in order to compensate investors for the risks involved. Typical examples are:

- *Ex-warrant* bonds: bonds issued with attached warrants, which have subsequently been *stripped* from the bond and sold on separately. The value of warrants to investors allows these bonds to be issued with low coupons. When warrants are stripped, the so-called **stub** of the issue goes into deep discount, in order to bring the yield on such bonds up to market levels by supplementing the low coupons with capital gains to be realised when the bond is repaid at face value at maturity. Deeply-discounted bonds tend to be unpopular with investors for a number of reasons, eg, income tax usually has to be paid on the return represented by the discount as it accrues, despite the fact that the discount does not yield an actual payment till maturity. The consequent illiquidity of ex-warrant bonds has, in practice, been aggravated by the sheer volume of bonds with warrants which were issued by Japanese borrowers on the back of the equity boom in Japan in the second-half of the 1980s and then stripped.

- *Asset-backed* securities, particularly collateralised mortgage obligations (CMOs): these securities suffer from the risk of prepayment of the underlying mortgages.

- *Highly-structured* securities: complex bonds targeted at narrow groups of investors with tailored, often innovative, risk features. These have proved too complex or too narrowly focused and have become illiquid.

- *Illiquid* issues: usually bonds which have been too aggressively priced at issue, weakly syndicated and poorly distributed (a common problem in the bond markets due to competitive pressures); or suffer from the quality of the issuer, the size of the issue and lack of market-makers. The spread over the relevant benchmark yield on such bonds widens at or after issue, sometimes dramatically, opening up arbitrage opportunities against swaps. Investors are willing to buy products synthesised from illiquid bonds, because the secondary market problems of the original bonds should be made irrelevant by swapping them into new synthetic securities.

- *Swap-driven* issues: some new issues are priced specifically to swap into synthetic FRNs. This route allows fixed-income issues by names not sufficiently creditworthy to gain direct access to the bond market. The feasibility of such issues essentially reflects the demand for floating-rate assets, particularly by banks, which have sought such securities as a substitute for high quality bank loans. The supply of loan assets has dwindled as the creditworthiness of banks was compromised after 1982 by the sovereign debt crisis and the availability and cost of credit was tightened. However, the supply of real FRNs was reduced in early 1986 by a number of major issuers exercising call options in order to switch to cheaper sources of funding (eg, Eurocommercial paper and Euronotes) and then by a collapse in the market at the end of the year, following a crisis in the perpetual FRN sector. Synthetic FRNs also provided an alternative supply of floating-rate US dollar assets to banks, particularly those entering the international markets in the second-half of the 1980s, most notably Japanese and Australian banks.

- As with liabilities, arbitrage opportunities with assets can arise because of variations in the *speed* at which different financial markets respond to the same information. For example, as explained previously, US Treasury securities react rapidly to news, whereas the US dollar bond market is somewhat slower. A rally in US Treasury prices will therefore tend to depress yields and swap rates (which are priced off Treasury yields) in advance of a similar response in bond yields. This opens up the possibility that bond issues can be bought at yields high enough relative to swap rates to allow arbitrage into high-yielding synthetic FRNs (refer back to Diagram 25).

Asset swaps are described in greater detail in the Workbook *Financial Engineering with Swaps*, which is part of The Swaps Series.

New issue arbitrage

It was explained that many (liability) swap arbitrages arise because of differences between the credit risk premia demanded from the same counterparty by cash markets and the swaps market. In fact, interest rate swaps were devised in order to realise credit risk arbitrage opportunities. Such opportunities are usually exploited to reduce the cost of new issues of debt. This type of swapping is therefore known as **new issue arbitrage**.

An example

Take two companies, one with a AA credit rating on its senior debt and the other with an A rating. Assume both companies, which will be called AA and A, respectively, can raise funds in the fixed-income bond market or through floating-rate bank loans at the costs set out in Table 4 below.

Table 4: Cost of capital market funds

	Fixed-income bonds	Floating-rate loans
Company AA	10%pa	Libor + 100bp
Company A	12%pa	Libor + 160bp
Differential	200bp	60bp

What is noticeable about the relative funding costs of the two companies is that AA can fund itself more cheaply than A by 200 basis points in the bond market, but by only 60 basis points from banks. The bond and credit markets clearly have very different perceptions of the relative credit risk of AA and A, in terms of the additional return required to compensate for the greater credit risk on A compared with AA.

This difference in the pricing of the relative credit risk of AA and A by different segments of the capital market can be exploited using an interest rate swap. Basically, AA borrows fixed-rate funds and swaps the interest cost in a way which splits the advantage with A. Because the arbitrage requires a swap, a prerequisite for the deal is that AA actually wants to end up with floating-rate funds and A actually wants to end up with fixed-rate. Assuming this is the case, the arbitrage requires the following steps.

Step 1   AA borrows fixed-rate funds by issuing a bond at 10% and A takes a bank loan at Libor plus 160bp.

Step 2   AA and A can swap with each other to leave AA paying a floating rate and A paying a fixed rate. In the swap, AA would be the receiver of fixed interest and A the payer. Assume the floating rate in the swap is the conventional Libor. The set of transactions is illustrated in Diagram 26 below.

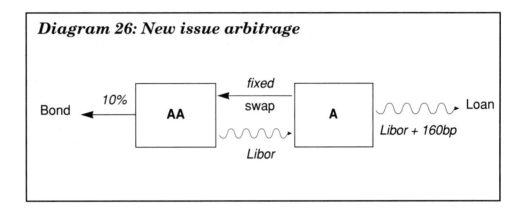

Diagram 26: New issue arbitrage

Step 3   If AA receives fixed interest through the swap at a rate higher than 10%, it will make a turn over the cost of its bond issue, which can subsidise the Libor it is paying through the swap, to produce a net cost of borrowing below Libor.

Step 4   On the other hand, A will make a loss by paying Libor plus 160bp on its bank loan and receiving only Libor through the swap. If A is to gain from the arbitrage, therefore, the fixed interest it pays through the swap should be at least 160 basis points cheaper than its cost of borrowing directly in the bond market. As A's cost of borrowing directly in the bond market is 12%pa, it needs a fixed rate in the swap of less than 10.40%pa (= 12% − 160bp).

Step 5   Exactly where the fixed rate in the swap should be set between 10% and 10.40% is a matter for AA and A to negotiate between themselves. Assume they agree on 10.20%pa. The net cost of funds for AA and A would be:

Table 5a: Net cost of funds to AA

Payments	fixed interest on bonds	@ 10.00%pa
	floating interest through swap	@ Libor
Receipts	fixed interest through swap	@ 10.20%pa
Net cost	floating interest	@ Libor – 20bp

Table 5b: Net cost of funds to A

Payments	floating interest on bank loan	@ Libor + 160bp
	fixed interest through swap	@ 10.20%pa
Receipts	floating interest through swap	@ Libor
Net cost	fixed interest	@ 11.80%pa

To summarise, AA has reduced the cost of its floating-rate funding by 120 basis points from Libor plus 100bp to Libor minus 20bp. A has reduced its cost of fixed-rate funding by 20 basis points from 12% to 11.80%. These gains are the result of AA and A acting in concert. The two companies together saved 200 basis points by having AA rather than A issue a bond, but lost 60 basis points by having A and not AA take out a bank loan, producing a net gain between them of 140 basis points (of which AA took 120 basis points and A took 20). Although A's borrowing made a loss, this was more than offset by the gain on AA's borrowing and it is essential to remember that AA cannot realise any gain without the swap with A.

There are a number of points to note about new issue arbitrage:

■ In the example above, it would be possible for the arbitrage to go ahead, even if A had no access to the bond market at all. After all, A does not have to enter the bond market: this is done by AA. All that is necessary is for A to have a target figure in mind for its net cost of funds. Interest rate swaps are, therefore, not only a method of reducing funding cost, but also a means of gaining *access* to bond markets or even of creating a *synthetic* bond market which would not otherwise be available to borrowers (possibly due to official restrictions or just the underdeveloped state of the financial markets in a particular currency).

■ Given the cost reductions which swap arbitrage can achieve, it is not surprising that swap opportunities are a crucial consideration in bond issuance. It has been estimated that about 70% of international bond issues are 'swap-driven', meaning the choice of market and timing of issuance are inspired by swap opportunities. The funding costs which swapped bond issues can achieve are, for AAA-rated sovereign borrowers, as low as Libor minus 60bp.

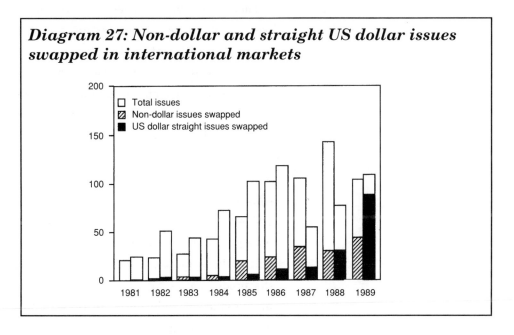

Diagram 27: Non-dollar and straight US dollar issues swapped in international markets

■ Differences in the pricing of the relative credit risk of two swap counterparties by different segments of the capital market indicate that information is not being equally distributed or assimilated across the bond and credit markets. The usual reason is that many bond markets have a large proportion of *retail investors*. They cannot undertake their own credit analysis. Because they are also particularly averse to credit risk, they tend to err on the side of creditworthiness when choosing investments. To tempt such investors into bonds with less than the best credit ratings, it is necessary to offer disproportionately more compensation for taking the same extra credit risk than would be required by wholesale investors, who typically undertake their own credit analysis. The importance of the retail element in a bond market is reflected in the fact that swap arbitrage is particularly important in largely retail bond markets such as those in Australian dollars and Swiss francs. It has been suggested that virtually 100% of international Australian dollar bond issues are swap-driven.

■ The mechanism at work in new issue arbitrage is similar to that proposed by the early 19th century English political economist David Ricardo to explain international trade. Ricardo used a two-country two-good model of the world economy, in which one country was more efficient at producing both goods than the other (just as AA in the example above can raise cheaper funds than A in both the bond and credit markets). Ricardo suggested that, if the 'efficient' country was not equally more efficient than the 'inefficient' country in producing both goods, it would be possible to realise an overall gain in welfare, if each country specialised in producing a different good and exchanged it for the other through trade. By specialising in its most efficient line of production, the efficient country should realise enough of a productivity gain to more than offset the loss of production through having the 'inefficient' country produce the other good. The inefficient country minimises this loss by specialising in its *least inefficient* line of production (just as A borrowed through a loan) and the efficient country maximises the offsetting gain by specialising in its *most efficient* line of production (just as AA borrowed through a bond). The efficient country is said to have an absolute advantage in the production of both goods, but a **comparative advantage** in the one it produces most efficiently, while the inefficient country has an absolute disadvantage in the production of both goods, but a comparative advantage in the one it produces least inefficiently. In the example above, AA has a comparative advantage in bonds and A has a comparative advantage in bank loans.

■ New issue arbitrage swaps were arranged initially by banks acting as agents for swap counterparties. However, corporate counterparties have traditionally been reluctant to take on the credit risk of other non-banks and banks have for some time been required to participate in swaps as principal intermediaries. The structure of a new issue arbitrage swap is therefore slightly more complicated than in the example demonstrated above. One swap becomes two, between the intermediary bank and each of the end-user counterparties. The intermediary bank acts like a swap dealer (as illustrated in Diagram 9 in *Part One*), charging for the credit risk it is taking in the form of a dealing spread between the fixed interest it receives and the fixed interest it pays. The structure of the new issue arbitrage swap demonstrated above would therefore probably be as illustrated in Diagram 28 below (assuming a 10 basis point spread to the intermediary bank).

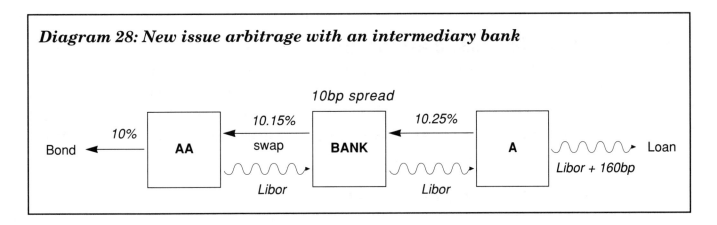

Diagram 28: New issue arbitrage with an intermediary bank

Typically, the demand for fixed-rate funds comes from A-rated borrowers, while that for floating-rate funds comes from AA-rated borrowers. Naturally, A-rated swap counterparties want to swap into fixed-rate funds at less than the typical yield on A-rated bonds. On the other hand, AA-rated counterparties want to subsidise their floating-rate interest payments with a turn between fixed interest received through the swap and the payments on their bond issues, which means the swap rates have to be higher than the yields on typical AA-rated bonds. As a consequence, as shown in Diagram 29 below, swap spreads tend to fluctuate within the 20–30 basis point range generally defined by the difference between the spreads over government yields on AA and A-rated corporate bonds.

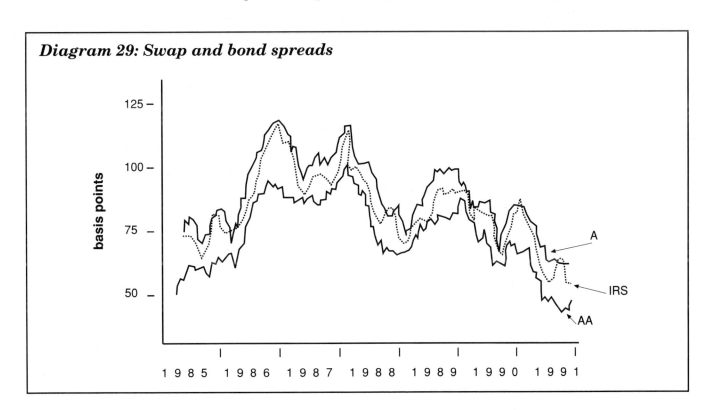

Diagram 29: Swap and bond spreads

Case study I: New issue arbitrage

The first publicised interest rate swap was used in a new issue arbitrage in December 1982 between Deutsche Bank Luxembourg and several smaller European banks. Deutsche Bank wanted cheap floating-rate dollars and the smaller European banks wanted cheap fixed-rate dollars. The cost of funds to the counterparties is not known for certain, except in the case of the funds actually borrowed. Other costs have been estimated and are set out in Table 6 below.

Table 6: Cost of capital market funds

	Fixed-income bonds	Floating rate loans
Deutsche Bank	11%pa	Libor
Other banks	12 1/8%pa	Libor + 5/8%
Differential	1 1/8%pa	5/8%pa

It is estimated that Deutsche Bank could have borrowed 1 1/8%pa cheaper than the smaller European banks in the fixed-income market, but only 5/8%pa cheaper in the floating-rate market. The comparative advantage in this situation was therefore 1/2%pa (= 1 1/8% − 5/8%). The steps in the swap were:

Step 1   Deutsche Bank Luxembourg issued a $110m seven-year bond at a coupon of 11%pa. The smaller European banks had access to floating-rate dollars at Libor plus 5/8%.

Step 2   Deutsche Bank Luxembourg and the smaller European banks swapped with each other, through the intermediary of CSFB and Merrill Lynch, to leave Deutsche Bank paying a floating rate and the smaller European banks paying a fixed rate. In the swap, Deutsche Bank was the receiver of fixed interest and the other banks were the payers. In this example, it is assumed that the floating rate in the swap was the conventional Libor. The set of transactions is illustrated in Diagram 30 below.

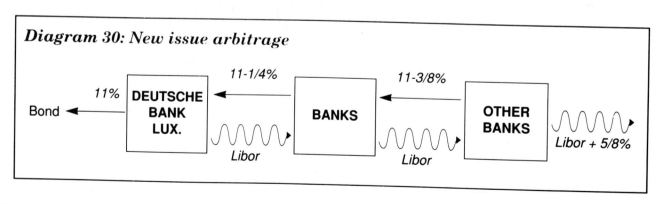

Diagram 30: New issue arbitrage

Step 3   Deutsche Bank needed to receive fixed interest through the swap at a rate higher than 11%pa, in order to make a turn over the cost of its bond issue with which to subsidise the Libor paid through the swap and so produce a net cost of borrowing below Libor.

Step 4   On the other hand, the smaller European banks made a loss, paying Libor plus 5/8% on their floating -rate dollars and receiving only Libor through the swap. To gain from the arbitrage, the smaller banks needed to pay fixed interest through the swap at a rate at least 5/8%pa cheaper than their cost of borrowing directly in the bond market, which would mean no more than 11 1/2%pa (= 12 1/8% – 5/8%).

Step 5   Exactly where the fixed rate in the swap was set between 11% and 11 1/2% would have been negotiated between Deutsche Bank and the other banks. Taking account of a dealing spread for the intermediary banks of 1/8%pa, the swap rates were set at 11 1/4%pa to be received by Deutsche Bank and 11 3/8%pa to have been paid by the smaller banks. In other words, it appears that Deutsche Bank took 1/2 or 1/4%pa of the gain and the other banks took 1/8%pa, leaving 1/8%pa for the intermediary banks. The net cost of funds for Deutsche Bank and the other banks would have been:

Table 7a: Net cost of funds to Deutsche Bank

Payments	fixed interest on bonds	@ 11.00%pa
	floating interest through swap	@ Libor
Receipts	fixed interest through swap	@ 11.25%pa
Net cost	floating interest	@ Libor – 25bp

Table 7b: Net cost of funds to the other banks

Payments	floating interest on bank loan	@ Libor + 5/8%
	fixed interest through swap	@ 11 3/8%pa
Receipts	floating interest through swap	@ Libor
Net cost	fixed interest	@ 12.00%pa

To summarise, Deutsche Bank reduced the cost of its floating-rate funding by 1/4%pa from Libor to Libor minus 25bp. The smaller banks reduced the cost of fixed-rate funding by 1/8%pa, from 12 1/8%pa to 12.00%pa. The two sides saved 1 1/8%pa by having Deutsche Bank rather than the smaller banks issue a bond, but lost 5/8%pa by having the smaller banks and not Deutsche Bank borrow floating-rate funds, producing a net gain between them of 1/2%pa (= 1 1/8% – 5/8%). Although the other banks' borrowing made a loss, this was more than offset by the gain on Deutsche Bank's borrowing.

Return management with swaps: arbitrage with other derivatives

The principle of arbitrage was defined in the previous section as a 'simultaneous sale and purchase of the same commodity at different prices to realise a profit'. In an arbitrage between derivatives, the 'commodity' being bought and sold is a net interest payment calculated from the differential between current and future rates of interest. For example, a coupon swap is an exchange of fixed interest calculated at the rate of interest prevailing at the time the swap was transacted against floating interest calculated at rates of interest prevailing on future dates. The resulting net interest payment is available, not only through swaps, but also in the alternative forms of **forward rate agreements (FRA) and interest rate futures**. If one instrument generates a higher rate of interest than another, but they both calculate interest using the same index, then it is possible to arbitrage by arranging to receive the higher rate and pay the lower rate. In an efficient market in which the markets in different derivatives have access to the same price information, the two rates should be the same. In practice, price discrepancies occur and give rise to arbitrage opportunities.

Arbitrage with FRAs

Interest rate risk can be hedged by buying an FRA (see *Box 1* for a brief introduction to FRAs). If the Settlement Rate on the FRA turns out to exceed the Contract Rate, the buyer receives a Net Compensation Amount related to the differential, which can be used to offset increased interest rates. If the Settlement Rate turns out to be below the Contract Rate, the buyer would pay the differential to the seller of the FRA. The overall interest rate exposure of the FRA buyer (and the seller) would therefore be fixed. Thus, if the buyer used the FRA to hedge a future borrowing, the profit or loss from the FRA would offset the increased or reduced cost of borrowing. Although an FRA only ever pays the difference between its Settlement and Contract Rates, it can be pictured as an exchange of gross interest based on these rates, as illustrated in Diagram 31 below. The Settlement Rate is floating, by virtue of the fact that it is not fixed till the end of the contract period, while the Contract Rate is fixed at the start of the FRA. It can therefore be seen that there is no essential functional difference between an FRA and a coupon swap. Note that the buyer of the FRA pays the Contract Rate (which is fixed) and receives the Settlement Rate (which floats); thus, a rise in the Settlement Rate above the Contract Rate will produce net payments to the buyer. This means that buying an FRA is equivalent to buying a swap, in that the buyer buys the right to pay fixed interest in both types of contract.

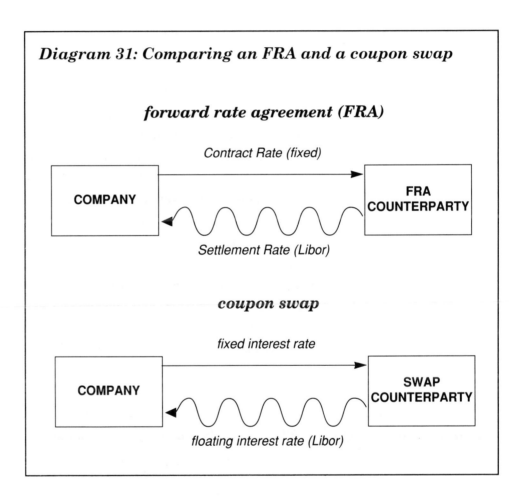

Diagram 31: Comparing an FRA and a coupon swap

forward rate agreement (FRA)

Contract Rate (fixed)

COMPANY — FRA COUNTERPARTY

Settlement Rate (Libor)

coupon swap

fixed interest rate

COMPANY — SWAP COUNTERPARTY

floating interest rate (Libor)

Given that FRAs and coupon swaps perform the same function, an FRA and an equivalent coupon swap should offer the same fixed rate of interest. If not, it should be possible to arbitrage between the two, as illustrated in Diagram 32 below, in which a fixed interest rate is paid through an FRA (ie, the FRA has been sold) and received through a coupon swap (ie, the swap has been bought).

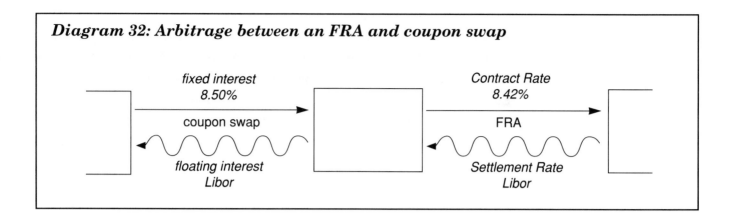

Diagram 32: Arbitrage between an FRA and coupon swap

Although there is no real functional difference between an FRA and an interest rate swap, there are practical differences which affect the way an arbitrage is transacted. Most importantly, an FRA covers only a single interest period, usually of three or six months, whereas an interest rate swap covers several such periods. To arbitrage FRAs against a swap, it is necessary to transact a **strip** or series of consecutive FRAs stretching over the life of the swap (but the initial period, from the present up to the first FRA contract, has to be covered in the cash market, as FRAs are for forward-forward periods only)[3]. An FRA strip is illustrated in Diagram 33 below. The Contract Rates on each of the FRAs are compounded to provide an average multi-period fixed interest rate. The arithmetic of 'stripping' is explained and demonstrated in *Part Four* on *Pricing and Valuing Swaps*. In practice, the length of FRA strips is constrained by the fact that most FRA markets are liquid only out to about 18 months (US dollar and sterling FRAs are liquid beyond two years).

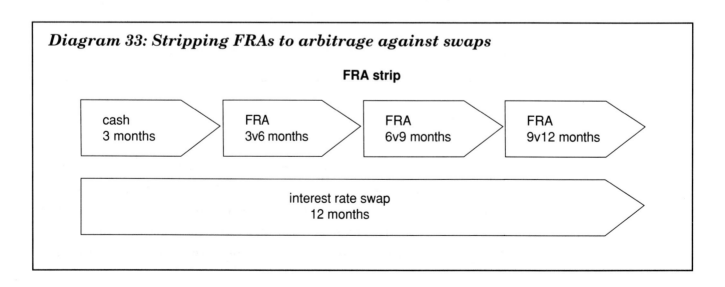

Diagram 33: Stripping FRAs to arbitrage against swaps

Box 1: Forward Rate Agreements

An FRA is a contract to pay the *difference* between the value of an agreed amount of a physical or financial commodity — which is to be notionally bought or sold at an agreed future date — calculated using a price fixed now and the value calculated using a price to be established on the agreed future date. The price fixed now is the *current forward* price for the commodity, meaning the price for its delivery on the agreed future date which is available in advance, when the FRA is transacted. The price to be established on the agreed future date is the *future cash* price for the commodity, meaning the price for its delivery which actually prevails when the agreed future date eventually comes around.

If the future cash price turns out to be less than the current forward price, the buyer of the FRA compensates the seller; and vice versa. Therefore, the buyer of an FRA gains, if prices in the future turn out to be higher than was indicated by earlier forward prices; and the seller gains, if prices in the future are lower; and vice versa. Note that only differences in value — called **Net Compensation Amounts** — are exchanged through FRAs, which are therefore sometimes described as **contracts for differences.**

Most FRAs are contracts for interest. Such contracts pay the difference between the interest due on an agreed amount of money — which is to be notionally loaned or borrowed at an agreed future date for an agreed term (ie, for an agreed foward-forward period) — calculated using an interest rate fixed now and the interest calculated using an interest rate to be established on the agreed future date. The interest rate fixed now is the *current forward-forward* interest rate for the agreed future term which is available in advance when the FRA is transacted. The interest rate to be established on the agreed future date is the *future cash* interest rate for the agreed term, meaning the interest rate which actually turns out to be prevailing when the start of the agreed term eventually comes around.

If the future cash interest rate turns out to be less than the current forward-forward interest rate, the buyer of the FRA compensates the seller; and vice versa. Therefore, the buyer of an FRA gains, if future interest rates turn out to be higher than was indicated by earlier forward-forward rates; and the seller gains, if future interest rates are lower; and vice versa. This means that borrowers hedge against interest rises by buying FRAs; and investors hedge against interest rate falls by selling FRAs.

The forward-forward periods covered by FRAs are usually described in terms of the number of months till the start of the period and the number of months till the end, eg, an FRA covering a three-month term starting in three months time is called a *3 against 6*. As the term in the example is three months, the interest rate would be of a three-month tenor (eg, three-month Libor). A *6 against 12* FRA, on the other hand, would involve an interest rate of a six-month tenor.

Note that only (net) interest payments are made through an FRA. Although an FRA pays the difference between the interest due on an agreed amount of money, this amount of money is a *notional* principal amount: it is used only for the calculation of interest. No principal changes hands in an FRA, which is therefore an *off-balance sheet* instrument. Borrowers or lenders hedging with FRAs do not have to borrow or invest with their FRA counterparties.

The current forward-forward interest rate in an FRA is called the **Contract Rate** and the future cash interest rate is called the **Settlement Rate**. The Contract Rate is fixed when the FRA is transacted; the Settlement Rate is fixed at the agreed future date. The Settlement Rate, where Libor is used in an FRA, is usually the British Bankers' Association Interest Rate Swap (BBAIRS) Interest Settlement Rate published daily on *Telerate* pages 3740–50 (see *Part Three* on *Trading Swaps*).

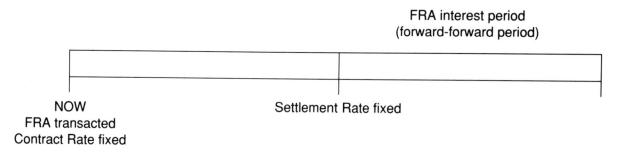

FRA interest period (forward-forward period)	
NOW FRA transacted Contract Rate fixed	Settlement Rate fixed

To minimise credit risk, an FRA pays a Net Compensation Amount as soon as the Settlement Rate is known, which is at the start of the interest period to which the rate applies. As interest rates assume payment at the *end* of the interest period to which they apply, the Net Compensation Amount is the differential between the Contract and Settlement Rates, applied to the notional principal amount of the FRA, *discounted* to take account of the fact it is paid on the contract date rather than the settlement date. The formula for calculating Net Compensation Amounts is:

$$\frac{I.D.NPA}{A\left(1+\left(L\left(\dfrac{D}{A}\right)\right)\right)}$$

Where

I	=	$R - L$, if $R > L$ or $L - R$, if $R < L$
R	=	Contract Rate (percentage rate divided by 100)
L	=	Settlement Rate (percentage rate divided by 100)
D	=	number of days in the forward–forward period
NPA	=	notional principal amount
A	=	number of days in the year

Arbitrage with futures

Arbitrage against coupon swaps is possible, not only with FRAs, but also with interest rate futures contracts. Interest rate futures are essentially standardised FRAs traded on a centralised exchange: a brief introduction to futures is given in *Box 2*. It is explained that short-term interest rate futures are quoted in terms of price, where price is equal to 100 minus the forward-forward interest rate for the contract period, eg, an interest rate of 8.5% would be reflected in a futures price of 91.50 (= 100 − 8.5). The price will move inversely to the underlying interest rate. The rules for using futures to hedge are therefore the opposite to those on instruments, such as FRAs and swaps, which are quoted in terms of interest rates. Thus, it is necessary to buy futures against an interest rate fall (the resulting increase in the futures' price will yield a hedging profit) and sell futures against an interest rate rise (to profit from a decrease in the futures' price). It will be recalled that FRAs are bought to hedge against the risk of interest rate rises and sold against the risk of interest rate falls (the same is true for swaps, where 'buying' a swap is equivalent to paying fixed and receiving floating interest and 'selling' a swap is the reverse).

Just as FRAs are stripped to produce an average multi-period fixed interest rate which can be compared to the fixed rate on a coupon swap, so too are futures. Again, as with FRAs, the length of futures strips are constrained by the fact that most futures contracts are liquid only out to about 18 months (three-month Eurodollar and sterling futures are liquid beyond two years). The arithmetic of a futures strip is demonstrated in *Part Four* on *Pricing and Valuing Swaps*.

Arbitrage with other derivatives

Besides FRAs and interest rate futures, it is possible to arbitrage interest rate swaps against other off-balance sheet and derivative instruments with interest rate effects, including foreign exchange swaps, synthetic agreements for forward exchange (SAFEs) and interest rate option products such as caps.

Monitoring swap arbitrage opportunities

Swap market participants continuously compare the prices of futures and FRAs strips against coupon swaps, in order to detect arbitrage opportunities. This comparison is typically performed on a real-time spreadsheet, which may be specially constructed by the user on a product such as *Telerate Matrix RTS* or may be monitored on a pre-prepared information screen of the type offered by *Thomson Financial Services (TFS)* on its *MoneyData* service disseminated on *Telerate*. Diagram 34 reproduces page 8066 from *MoneyData*.

Diagram 34: Arbitrage data on a screen page

		MONEYDATA TFS (C) 92		US INT RATE SWAPS & FRAS		10/29	10:34	8066
[TSY-BEY]	[SWAP A/360-HI/LO]	STUB TO 12/16/92		3.28		[IMM EURO$]		
1YR	3.44	3.89	3.90/88	[SEMI 30/360]	[SPRD-HI/LO]		Z92	96.40	Z93	94.90
2YR	4.29	4.65		4.67	38	39/37	H93	96.40	H94	94.67
3YR	4.75	5.29		5.29	54	57/53	M93	95.95	M94	94.30
4YR	5.27	5.78		5.77	50	53/48	U93	95.52	U94	94.01
5YR	5.79	6.15		6.14	35	38/33			Z94	93.60
		[FRA BREAKEVENS (IMPLIED BY IMM STRIP)]					H95	93.49
[CASH LIBOR]			3MO		6MO		12MO		M95	93.27
O/N	3.00	1X4	3.61	1X7	3.62	1X13	ERR	U95	93.11
1MO	3.25	2X5	3.59	2X8	3.65	2X14	ERR	Z95	92.83
2MO	3.31	3X6	3.60	3X9	3.74	3X15	4.20	H96	92.80
3MO	3.63	4X7	3.60	4X10	3.81	4X16	4.34	M96	92.62
4MO	3.63	5X8	3.68	5X11	3.92	5X17	4.47	U96	92.49
6MO	3.63	6X9	3.83	6X12	4.08	6X18	4.61	Z96	92.29
9MO	3.75	9X12	4.28	9X15	4.57	9X21	5.03	H97	92.33
12MO	3.94	12X15	4.81	12X18	5.04	12X24	5.15	M97	92.19
								U97	92.09

NOTE: (I) - FOUR YEAR TSY IS INTERPOLATED YLD.

Box 2: Short-term interest rate futures

A future is a contract which is available only with standard terms and conditions, and is traded on a centrally-organised exchange. A futures contract commits the counterparty buying the contract to:

■ actually or notionally buy — at an agreed price — a standard physical or financial commodity;

■ in an agreed multiple of a standard amount;

■ on one of a number of standard dates in the future.

Where a futures contract is only a commitment to notionally buy or sell, there is no physical delivery: a cash payment is made of the difference between the buying and selling price of the contract. Like an FRA, such futures contracts are therefore **contracts for differences**.

Unlike FRAs, futures contracts can be **closed out** (cancelled) before the date on which settlement is required. An outstanding contract is closed out by an opposite transaction in the same contract (ie, for the same commodity, same amount and same future delivery date). The difference between the buying and selling prices of the opposite contracts is settled in cash immediately.

An interest rate future is a contract which pays the difference between the interest due on the amount of money specified in the contract — which is to be notionally borrowed or loaned at an agreed future date for a fixed term (ie, for a forward-forward period) — where the interest is calculated using:

■ an interest rate fixed now; and

■ an interest rate to be established subsequently, within the period up to and including the agreed future date.

The interest rate which is fixed now should be the *current forward-forward* interest rate for the fixed term, meaning the rate for that term which is available in the futures market at the time the contract is transacted (eg, the interest rate for the term 15 September to 15 December which is fixed by transacting a futures contract on, say, 30 June). In practice, futures are driven by direct market expectations of future interest rates and may diverge from forward-forward rates.

The interest rate to be established subsequently depends on whether the contract is (1) closed out before or (2) left in place until the start of the fixed term (ie, 15 September). If the contract is closed out before the start of the fixed term (eg, on 8 July), the 'subsequent' interest rate is the forward-forward rate for the fixed term which is prevailing in the futures market when the outstanding contract is closed out (ie, the interest rate for the term 15 September to 15 December prevailing on 8 July). If the contract is left in place until start of the fixed term, the 'subsequent' interest rate is the *cash* interest rate for the fixed term which actually turns out to be prevailing when the fixed term eventually starts (ie, on 15 September).

Futures contracts are only available for a limited number of fixed terms each year: usually just four a year; and usually between mid-December, mid-March, mid-June and mid-September (for contracts traded on Liffe, mid-month means the third Wednesday).

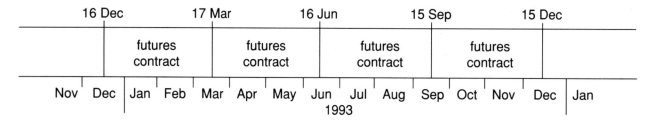

These standard contract periods, like the standard contract amounts, make it difficult to use futures to hedge actual interest rate exposures. There are usually mismatches in periods and amounts, and these create *basis risk* for users of futures. However, standardisation helps concentrate trading activity and thereby enhances the liquidity of futures contracts.

Most futures are priced in the same units as the commodities on which they are written, eg, gold futures are priced in US dollars per ounce, sterling/US dollar futures in sterling per US dollar and bond futures in percent of the face value of bonds. However, short-term interest rate futures are priced as the difference between 100 and the forward-forward interest rates on which the contracts are being written. Thus, if the three-month Eurodollar forward-forward interest rate for a period of mid-December to mid-March is currently 9.57% per annum, the current price of the futures contract should be 100 minus 9.57 = 90.43.

Given the method of pricing short-term interest rate futures relative to 100, it can be seen that a buyer of such a futures contract will profit, if interest rates fall, as this will increase the price of the contract. A seller will profit, if interest rates rise, as this will reduce the price of the contract. Therefore, borrowers hedge against interest rises by selling futures and investors hedge against interest rate falls by buying futures. It can be seen that the price of short-term interest rate futures behave like the price of fixed-income bonds, in being inversely related to yield.

Note that only (net) interest payments are made. Although a futures contract pays the difference between the interest due on a certain amount of money, this amount of money is a *notional* principal amount: it is used only for the calculation of interest. No principal changes hands in a future, which is therefore an *off-balance sheet* instrument. Borrowers or lenders hedging with futures do not borrow from or invest with their futures counterparties.

Notes

1. It is assumed that there is no *basis risk* between the floating rates on different sides of the balance sheet.

2. In this example, it is assumed that interest rates are quoted on the same basis, having been adjusted to take account of different calendar, compounding and coupon payment conventions.

3. The process of stripping FRAs should be distinguished from 'stripping' as used in the capital market, which means the separation of coupons from a fixed-income security in order to produce a zero-coupon bond.

Self-Study Exercises: <u>Questions</u>   Part 2

Question 2.1:   In the coupon swap illustrated below, which counterparty loses if interest rates rise over the life of the swap and which counterparty gains?

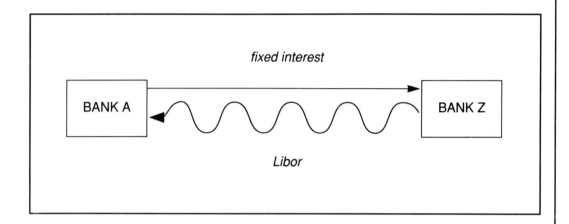

Question 2.2:   A company has borrowed through a floating-rate syndicated loan to take advantage of an expected fall in interest rates. After a period of falling rates, expectations change and a rise in interest rates is foreseen. If the company decides to hedge its exposure to a fall in rates with an interest rate swap, what should it pay or receive through the swap?

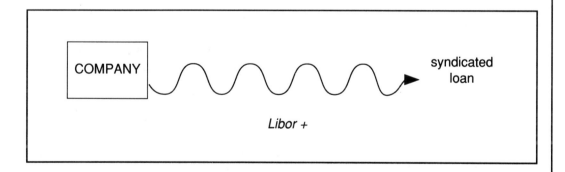

Question 2.3:   How would an interest rate swap be used to construct a *synthetic FRN* for an investor from a fixed-interest security?

Question 2.4: A financial institution has a balance sheet with fixed-interest assets broadly matched by fixed-interest liabilities. The institution is confident that interest rates will fall and decides to take a risk position on the basis of its expectations, using interest rate swaps. What should it pay or receive through the swap?

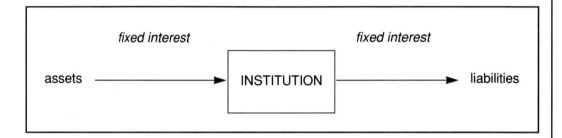

Question 2.5: A financial institution has a balance sheet with floating-interest assets broadly matched by floating-interest liabilities. The institution is confident that interest rates will fall and decides to take a risk position on the basis of its expectations, using interest rate swaps. What should it pay or receive through the swap?

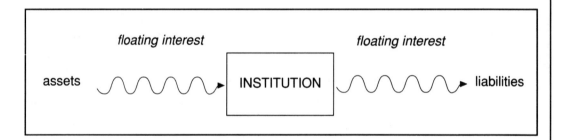

Question 2.6: A financial institution has a balance sheet with floating-interest assets, but fixed-interest liabilities. The institution is confident that interest rates will fall and decides to take a risk position on the basis of its expectations, using interest rate swaps. What should it pay or receive through the swap?

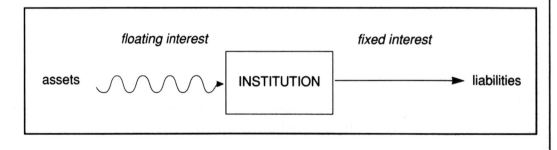

Question 2.7: A UK building society wants to fund its floating-interest mortgages by issuing fixed-income securities. What would be its interest rate risk? How would it use interest rate swaps to hedge this exposure? What should it pay or receive through the swap?

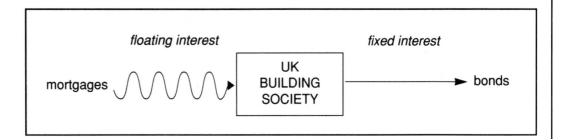

Question 2.8: A UK building society, funding itself with floating-interest deposits, wants to offer fixed-rate mortgages. What should be its interest rate risk? How could it use interest rate swaps to hedge this exposure? What should it pay or receive through the swap?

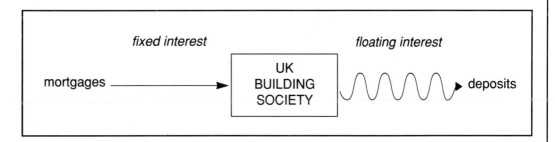

Question 2.9: A bank has transacted a *basis swap* between three-month and six-month Libor, in which it pays six-month Libor and receives three-month Libor. If the yield curve rotates clockwise and becomes inverted, does the bank gain or lose?

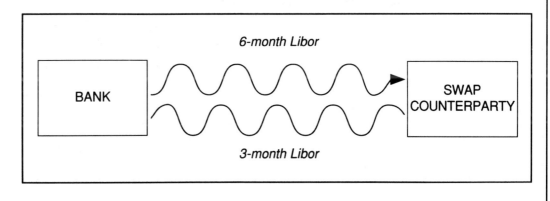

Question 2.10: An institution believes it can issue five-year fixed-interest securities at a yield of 10.625%pa, but would prefer to raise floating-interest funds. Five-year coupon swaps are being quoted at all-in rates of 10.75–10.875%pa (all rates are quoted on the same basis). If the institution wished to swap the proceeds of a bond issue, how would it use a coupon swap to do this: should it pay or receive fixed interest through the swap? What would be the all-in cost of its borrowing after swapping?

Question 2.11: An institution invested in an FRN, with a remaining period to maturity of three years, yielding Libor plus 100 basis points, but expects interest rates to fall and wishes to swap into fixed-interest funds using a coupon swap. Three-year swaps are trading at all-in rates of 9.625–9.75%pa (all rates are quoted on the same basis). How can it use a coupon swap to do this: should it pay or receive fixed interest through the swap? What would be the all-in return on its investment after swapping?

Question 2.12: If US dollar interest rates rise very rapidly, how can borrowers considering the issuance of fixed-interest securities use coupon swaps in arbitrages to reduce the cost of their borrowing?

Question 2.13: If US dollar interest rates fall very rapidly, how can investors in fixed-interest securities use coupon swaps in arbitrages to enhance the return on their investments?

Question 2.14: Interbank is investigating the possibility of arranging a *new issue arbitrage* between Anderson PLC and Zephyr (UK) Ltd. The estimated costs of borrowing for the two companies in the fixed and floating-interest markets are summarised in the table below (all rates are quoted on the same basis). Anderson wishes to raise floating-interest sterling and Zephyr fixed-interest. Assume that Interbank would act as a principal intermediary in a swap, for which it would charge each counterparty a spread of 7.5 basis points. Anderson has set a target for the cost of swapped funds of Libor, while Zephyr wants a gain of at least 10 basis points from the swap, which would reduce its cost of funds to 11.40% per annum. Can Interbank arrange a swap which satisfies the requirements of all parties? What would be the price of the swap, if it is feasible?

Cost of funds	Fixed-interest	Floating-interest
Anderson PLC	10.50%	Libor + 25bp
Zephyr (UK)	11.50%	Libor + 75bp

Question 2.15: IBC Bank is investigating the possibility of arranging a *new issue arbitrage* between Associated Corp. and Zimmerman Inc. The estimated costs of borrowing for the two companies in the fixed and floating-interest markets in US dollars are summarised in the table below (all rates are quoted on the same basis). Associated wishes to raise floating-interest dollars and Zimmerman fixed-interest. Assume that IBC Bank would act as a principal intermediary, for which it would charge each counterparty a spread of 5 basis points. Associated has set a target for the cost of swapped funds of Libor + 75 basis points, while Zimmerman wants a gain of at least 12.5 basis points from the swap, which would reduce its cost of funds to 12.25% per annum. Can IBC arrange a swap which satisfies the requirements of all parties? What would be the price of the swap, if it is feasible?

Cost of funds	Fixed-interest	Floating-interest
Associated	11.75%	Libor + 100bp
Zimmerman	12.375%	Libor + 125bp

Question 2.16: Infirst Bancorp is investigating the possibility of arranging a new issue arbitrage between Arlington International and Zona Bank. The estimated costs of borrowing for the two companies in the fixed and floating-interest markets are summarised in the table below (all rates are quoted on the same basis). Arlington wishes to raise floating-interest funds and Zona fixed-interest funds, both in sterling. Assume that Infirst would act as a principal intermediary, for which it would charge each counterparty a spread of 4 basis points. Arlington has set a target for the cost of swapped funds of Libor, while Zona wants a gain of at least 10 basis points from the swap. What would be the price of the swap, if it is feasible?

Cost of funds	Fixed-interest	Floating-interest
Arlington	4.50%	Libor + 25bp
Zona Bank	5.00%	Libor + 75bp

Question 2.17: A bank has transacted a coupon swap in which it pays fixed interest. It wishes to *warehouse* the swap, until it can find a matching swap, using its FRA book. Does it need to have short (net seller) or long positions (net buyer) in FRAs to hedge the swap?

Interest rate swaps

Question 2.18: A bank has transacted a sterling coupon swap in which it receives fixed interest. It wishes to *warehouse* the swap, until it can find a matching swap, with gilt futures. Should it buy or sell gilt futures? Why might the bank prefer gilt futures to gilt-edged securities?

Question 2.19: What are the differences between interest rate swaps and FRAs? Identify which of each pair of characteristics applies to which of the two instruments.

- extends over (A) *single* or (B) *multiple* interest period(s)
- is traded (C) *over the counter* or on (D) an *exchange*
- pays return (E) *gross* or (F) *net*
- is a (G) *standardised* or (H) *customised* contract
- is (I) free or is (J) subject to *capital requirements*
- can be (K) *closed out* before maturity or (L) only *reversed*
- are (M) *cash* or (N) *derivative* instruments
- *settle* at the (O) start or (P) end of interest periods

Question 2.20: What are the differences between interest rate swaps and futures contracts? Identify which of each pair of characteristics applies to which of the two instruments.

- extends over (A) *single* or (B) *multiple* interest period(s)
- is traded (C) *over the counter* or on (D) an *exchange*
- pays return (E) *gross* or (F) *net*
- is a (G) *standardised* or (H) *customised* contract
- is (I) free or is (J) subject to *capital requirements*
- can be (K) *closed out* before maturity or (L) only *reversed*
- are (M) *cash* or (N) *derivative* instruments
- *settle* at the (O) start or (P) end of interest periods

Self-Study Exercises: <u>Answers</u>   Part 2

Answer 2.1: If interest rates rise over the life of the swap illustrated in Question 2.1, *Bank A* — which is the payer of fixed interest and receiver of floating — will gain because an interest rate increase will increase the floating interest it receives through the swap, while its payments are fixed. Bank Z will lose.

Answer 2.2: If the company in Question 2.2 believes interest rates will rise, it should fix the rate of interest it pays on its borrowing. To do this with a swap, it should put on a coupon swap in which it *pays* fixed interest and receives floating. The floating interest received through the swap would be used to fund floating payments due on the syndicated loan, leaving the company paying fixed interest through the swap. It will have converted its syndicated loan to a *synthetic* fixed-interest liability.

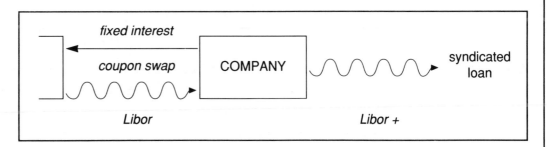

Answer 2.3: A synthetic FRN is constructed by putting on a coupon swap in which an investor in a fixed-interest security *pays* fixed interest through the swap and receives floating. The fixed interest on the real security is used to fund the fixed interest paid through the swap, leaving the investor in receipt of the floating interest paid by the swap. Thus, although the investor holds a fixed-interest security, he or she is receiving floating interest.

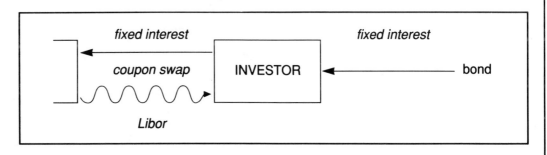

Answer 2.4:   If the institution in Question 2.4 believes interest rates will fall, it should keep the return on its assets fixed, but convert its payments to floating interest rates to benefit from lower rates. To do this with a swap, it should put on a coupon swap in which it *receives* fixed interest and pays floating. The fixed interest received through the swap is used to fund the fixed interest due on the liabilities, leaving the institution receiving fixed interest on its assets and paying floating interest through the swap.

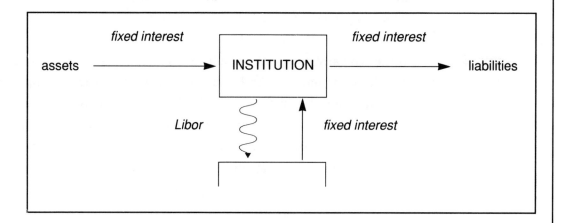

Answer 2.5:   If the institution in Question 2.5 believes interest rates will fall, it should keep the payments on its liabilities at floating interest rates, in order to benefit from a fall in rates, but should fix the return on its assets. To do this with a swap, it should put on a coupon swap in which it *receives* fixed interest and pays floating. The floating interest paid on its assets is used to fund the floating interest paid through the swap, leaving the institution receiving fixed interest through the swap and paying floating interest through the swap.

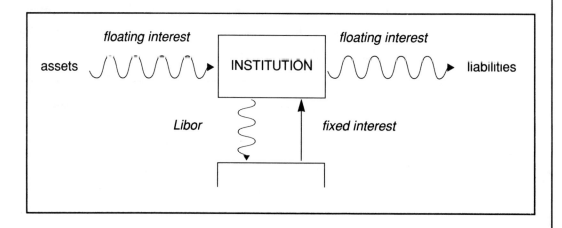

Answer 2.6: If the institution in Question 2.6 believes interest rates will fall, it should either fix the return on its assets or convert its liabilities to a floating interest rate or both. To do this with a swap, it should put on a coupon swap in which it *receives* fixed interest and pays floating. The floating interest received on its assets is used to fund the floating interest paid through the swap and the fixed interest received through the swap is used to fund the fixed interest due on the liabilities. However, if the notional principal amount of the swap only matches the principal amount of the institution's assets and liabilities, the swap merely hedges against a fall in interest rates and the institution will make no gain if rates fall. To do this, additional swaps need to be put, so that the institution becomes a net receiver of fixed interest and a net payer of floating.

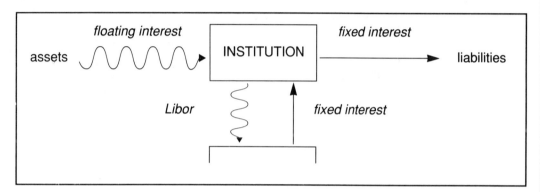

Answer 2.7: The building society in Question 2.7 is exposed to the risk that interest rates will *fall*, as this would reduce the interest received on its mortgages, while the interest paid on its bonds would remain fixed. To hedge against a fall in rates, the building society should either fix the return on its mortgages or convert its bonds into synthetic floating-interest instruments (FRNs) or both. To do this with a swap, it should put on a coupon swap in which it *receives* fixed interest and pays floating. The floating interest paid on its mortgages is used to fund the floating interest paid through the swap and the fixed interest received through the swap is used to fund the fixed interest due on its bonds.

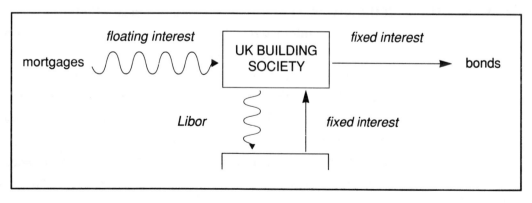

Answer 2.8: The building society in Question 2.8 is exposed to the risk that interest rates will *rise*, as this would increase the interest due on its deposits, while the interest received on its mortgages would remain fixed. To hedge against a rise in rates, the building society should fix the interest rate on its deposits or convert its mortgages to floating interest rates or both. To do this with a swap, it should put on a coupon swap in which it *pays* fixed interest and receives floating. The fixed interest paid through the swap is funded with the fixed interest received on its mortgages and the floating interest received through the swap is used to fund the floating interest due on its deposits.

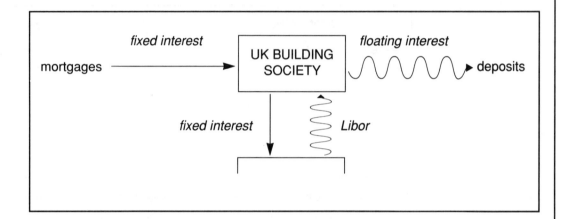

Answer 2.9: If the yield curve rotates clockwise and becomes inverted, the level of three-month Libor would exceed six-month Libor. The bank in Question 2.9 would therefore *gain* as it receives three-month Libor and pays six-month.

Answer 2.10: If the institution in Question 2.10 issues a fixed-interest security, it can convert it to a floating interest rate by putting on a coupon swap in which it *receives* fixed interest and pays floating: the fixed interest received through the swap is used to fund the fixed interest due on the bond issue, leaving the institution paying floating interest through the swap at Libor. It will have converted its bonds into *synthetic* floating-rate notes (FRNs). They can put on a swap at 10.75% (the swap market is seeking to pay 10.75% and receive 10.875%) and pay floating (at Libor). Given that the institution can issue a bond at 10.625% per annum, it would make a 12.5 basis point per annum profit (the difference between the 10.75% received through the swap and the 10.625% paid on the bond issue). This profit is used to subsidise the Libor which the institution is left paying through the swap. Thus, the all-in cost of its borrowing after swapping would be Libor minus 12.5 basis points.

cost of bond	−10.625%
fixed receipts through swap	+10.75%
floating payments through swap	− Libor
all-in cost of borrowing	− Libor −12.5bp

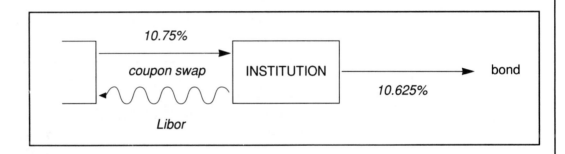

Answer 2.11: If the institution in Question 2.11 puts on a coupon swap in which it *receives* fixed interest and pays floating, it can use the floating interest from its FRN to fund the floating interest paid through the swap, leaving it receiving fixed interest. The institution can put on a swap through which it receives 9.625% (the swap market is seeking to pay 9.625% and receive 9.75%) and pays floating (at Libor). Given that the institution receives Libor plus 100 basis points on its FRN, it would make a 100 basis point per annum profit by swapping (the difference between the Libor plus 100 basis points received on the FRN and the Libor paid through the swap). This profit is added to the 9.625% which the institution receives through the swap. Thus, the all-in return on its investment after swapping would be 10.625% per annum.

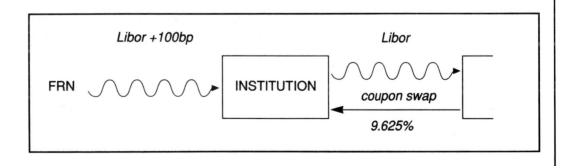

Answer 2.12: When interest rates change very rapidly, different markets respond at different speeds. In the US dollar market, the price of US Treasury securities typically changes faster than the price of US dollar Eurobonds. A rapid rise in US dollar interest rates would usually mean that the differential between US Treasury yields and Eurobond yields would widen. Swap rates would reflect US Treasury yields and so a differential will open up between swap rates and Eurobond yields. In these circumstances, the interest received on swaps may rise above the interest paid out on Eurobonds. By issuing Eurobonds and putting on a swap in which they receive fixed interest, borrowers can exploit that fact and realise a profit which can be used to subsidise the cost of their borrowing. As the fixed interest received through the swap largely offsets the fixed interest paid on the Eurobond, the borrower is left paying floating interest and in effect has a synthetic FRN.

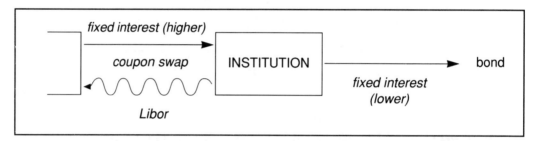

Answer 2.13: When interest rates change very rapidly, different markets respond at different speeds. In the US dollar market, the price of US Treasury securities typically changes faster than the price of US dollar Eurobonds. A rapid fall in US dollar interest rates would usually mean that the differential between US Treasury yields and Eurobond yields would widen. Swap rates would reflect US Treasury yields and so a differential will open up between swap rates and Eurobond yields. In these circumstances, the interest paid through swaps may fall below the interest paid out on Eurobonds. By investing in Eurobonds and putting on a swap in which they pay fixed interest, investors can exploit that fact and realise a profit which can be used to enhance the return on its investment. As the fixed interest paid through the swap largely offsets the fixed interest received on the Eurobond, the investor is left receiving floating interest and in effect has a synthetic FRN.

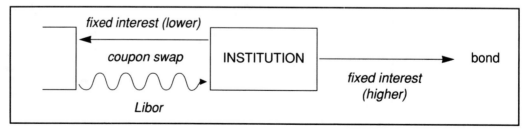

Answer 2.14: From the table in Question 2.14, it can be seen that Anderson can borrow fixed-interest funds 100 basis points more cheaply than Zephyr, but floating-interest funds would only be 50 basis points cheaper. The *comparative advantage* in this relationship is therefore 50 basis points (= 100 – 50 basis points).

Cost of funds	Fixed-interest	Floating-interest
Anderson PLC	10.50%	Libor + 25bp
Zephyr (UK)	11.50%	Libor + 75bp
difference	1.00% (100bp)	50bp

Anderson has a comparative advantage in fixed-interest funds and Zephyr in floating-interest funds. The swap would therefore require Anderson to raise fixed-interest funds and swap into floating-interest, and vice versa for Zephyr. As Anderson does want floating-interest funds and Zephyr does want fixed-interest funds, the swap makes sense in principle.

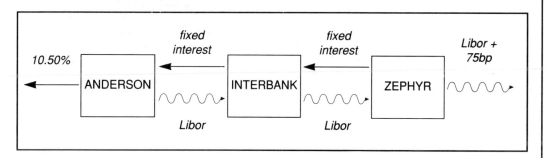

It is necessary to check if the comparative advantage of 50 basis points in the relationship between Anderson and Zephyr is sufficient to accommodate the reduction in borrowing costs which the two counterparties are seeking and the dealing spread which Interbank charges. Anderson wants to end up with floating-interest funds at Libor: as it can borrow directly at Libor plus 25 basis points, this means it will absorb at least 25 basis points of the comparative advantage. Zephyr wants to gain 10 basis points. Interbank charges *each* counterparty 7.5 basis points, taking a total of 15. In total, therefore, comparative advantage needs to be at least 50 basis points to satisfy all parties. The comparative advantage calculated from the table of borrowing costs is 50 basis points, so a swap should produce reductions in the cost of borrowing which satisfy both counterparties and generate a dealing spread which satisfies Interbank.

The next step is to calculate the swap rate, in other words the rate of fixed interest through the swap. The interest cash flows involved in the transaction are summarised for each counterparty in the following tables.

Interest cash flows to and from Anderson		
PAYMENTS	floating interest through swap	Libor
	fixed interest funds	10.50%
RECEIPTS	fixed interest through swap	?
NET COST	net floating interest	Libor

Interest cash flows to and from Zephyr		
PAYMENTS	fixed interest through swap	?
	floating interest funds	Libor + 75
RECEIPTS	floating interest through swap	Libor
NET COST	net fixed interest	11.40%

For the tables to balance, Anderson must receive fixed interest through the swap of *10.50%*pa and Zephyr must pay floating interest through the swap of *10.65%*pa. The 15 basis points difference is the dealing spread paid to Interbank. Interbank would therefore quote the price of the swap as 10.50–10.65% (meaning that it will pay fixed interest at 10.50% and seek 10.65%).

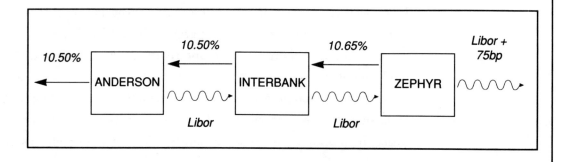

Answer 2.15:   From the table in Question 2.15, it can be seen that Associated can borrow fixed-interest funds 67.5 basis points more cheaply than Zimmerman, but floating-interest funds would only be 25 basis points cheaper. The *comparative advantage* in this relationship is therefore 37.5 basis points (= 62.5 – 25 basis points).

Cost of funds	Fixed-interest	Floating-interest
Associated	11.75%	Libor + 100bp
Zimmerman	12.375%	Libor + 125bp
difference	0.625% (62.5bp)	25bp

Associated has a comparative advantage in fixed-interest funds and Zimmerman in floating-interest funds. The swap would therefore require Associated to raise fixed-interest funds and swap into floating-interest, and vice versa for Zimmerman. As Associated does want floating-interest and Zimmerman does want fixed-interest funds, the swap makes sense in principle.

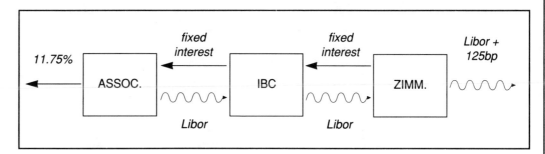

It is necessary to check if the comparative advantage of 37.5 basis points in the relationship between Associated and Zimmerman is sufficient to accommodate the reduction in borrowing costs which the two counterparties are seeking and the dealing spread which Interbank charges. Associated wants to end up with floating-interest funds at Libor plus 75 basis points: as it can borrow directly at Libor plus 100 basis points, this means it will absorb at least 25 basis points of the comparative advantage. Zimmerman wants to gain 12.5 basis points. IBC charges *each* counterparty 5 basis points, taking a total of 10. In total, therefore, comparative advantage needs to be at least 47.5 basis points (= 25 + 12.5 + 10) to satisfy all parties. The comparative advantage calculated from the table of borrowing costs is however only 37.5 basis points, so a swap will not produce reductions in the cost of borrowing which would satisfy both counterparties and generate a dealing spread that satisfies IBC.

Answer 2.16: From the table in Question 2.16, it can be seen that Arlington can borrow both fixed and floating-interest funds 50 basis points more cheaply than Zimmerman. This means that there is no *comparative advantage* in this relationship and no opportunity for a profitable swap.

Cost of funds	Fixed-interest	Floating-interest
Arlington	4.50%	Libor + 25bp
Zona Bank	5.00%	Libor + 75bp
difference	0.50% (50bp)	50bp

The lack of a swap opportunity can be demonstrated by trying to construct a swap.

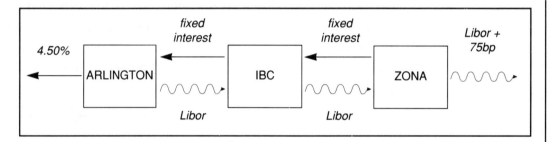

Interest cash flows to and from Arlington		
PAYMENTS	floating interest through swap	Libor
	fixed interest funds	4.50%
RECEIPTS	fixed interest through swap	?
NET COST	net floating interest	Libor

Interest cash flows to and from Zona		
PAYMENTS	fixed interest through swap	?
	floating interest funds	Libor + 75
RECEIPTS	floating interest through swap	Libor
NET COST	net fixed interest	4.90%

For the tables to balance, Arlington must receive fixed interest through the swap of *at least 4.50%* per annum and Zona must pay floating interest through the swap of *no more than 4.15%* per annum. If Arlington receives less than 4.50% per annum through the swap or Zona pays more than 4.15% per annum through the swap, then the cost of borrowing will rise above their targets. It can be seen from the tables that if Arlington received 4.50% per annum through the swap then the net cost of fixed-interest funds to Zona after the swap would be 5.25% per annum, above its direct cost of borrowing of 5.00% per annum. On the other hand, if Zona paid 4.15% per annum through the swap, the net cost of floating-interest funds to Arlington after the swap would be Libor plus 35 basis points, above its direct cost of borrowing of Libor plus 25 basis points. If Arlington received and Zona paid 4.25% per annum through the swap, the cost of floating-interest funds to Arlington after the swap would be Libor plus 25 basis points and the cost of fixed-interest funds to Zona after the swap would be 5.00% per annum — exactly the same as their direct costs of borrowing. In all these cases, there would be no dealing spread for IBC. In other words, there is no profitable swap opportunity between Arlington and Zona.

Answer 2.17:   A warehouse is another term for a hedge. The bank in Question 2.17 pays fixed interest through the swap. The risk which the bank wishes to hedge is that interest rates will fall, so that, by the time it arranges a matching swap through which it receives fixed interest, it will be receiving fixed interest at a lower rate through one swap than it is paying out through another. To hedge against this risk with FRAs, it would *sell* or *go short*.

This can be looked at in another way. To hedge the swap, the bank needs an equal and opposite interest rate exposure. As it is paying interest through the swap, hedging involves receiving fixed interest. An FRA can be seen as a swap between its Contract Rate and Settlement Rate. The Contract Rate is fixed when the FRA is negotiated and is therefore a fixed interest rate, while the Settlement Rate is uncertain until settlement and is therefore a floating rate. This means that FRAs are similar to coupon swaps. As the buyer of an FRA profits if interest rates rise, it is effectively paying fixed and receiving floating interest (an interest rate rise would increase interest receipts, while interest payments would remain fixed), ie, it pays interest at the fixed Contract Rate and receives interest at the floating Settlement Rate. As the bank in Question 2.17 is paying fixed interest through the swap, it should hedge by receiving fixed interest through FRAs, which means selling them.

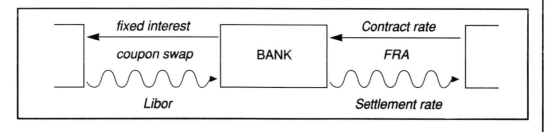

Answer 2.18: A warehouse is another term for a hedge. The bank in Question 2.18 receives fixed interest through the swap. The risk which the bank wishes to hedge is that interest rates will rise, so that, by the time it arranges a matching swap through which it pays fixed interest, it will be paying fixed interest at a higher rate through one swap than it is receiving through another. To hedge against this risk with gilt futures, it would *sell* or *go short*. If interest rates did rise, the price of gilts and gilt futures would fall: gilt futures could be bought, at a lower price, to close out the short position at a profit and compensate for the loss on the matching swap.

This can be looked at in another way. To hedge the swap, the bank needs an equal and opposite interest rate exposure. As it is receiving fixed interest through the swap, hedging involves paying fixed interest. A futures contract can be seen as a swap between the interest rate implied by the selling price and the interest rate implied by the buying price. In the futures hedge described above, the selling price is fixed when the futures are sold, implying a fixed interest rate, while the buying price is uncertain until the short position is closed out, therefore implying a floating rate. This means that futures contracts are similar to coupon swaps. As the seller of a futures contract profits if interest rates rise (as this depresses futures prices), it is effectively paying fixed and receiving floating interest (an interest rate rise would increase interest receipts, while interest payments would remain fixed). As the bank in Question 2.18 is receiving fixed interest through the swap, it should hedge by paying implied fixed interest through futures, which means selling futures.

The bank in Question 2.18 might prefer gilt futures to gilt-edged securities because it could not go short of gilt-edged securities, unless it was a Gilt-Edged Market-Maker authorised by the Bank of England. There are no such restrictions on selling gilts futures.

Answer 2.19:

	Interest rate swaps	FRAs
■ interest periods	B *multiple*	A *single*
■ traded	C *over the counter*	C *over the counter*
■ pays interest	E *gross or net*	F *net*
■ contract is	H *customised*	H *customised*
■ capital is	J *required*	J *required*
■ before maturity	L *only reversal*	L *only reversal*
■ instrument is	N *derivative*	N *derivative*
■ settles at	P *end of interest periods*	O *start of interest period*

Answer 2.20:

	Interest rate swaps	Futures
■ interest periods	B *multiple*	A *single*
■ traded	C *over the counter*	D *exchange*
■ pays return	E *gross or net*	F *net*
■ contract is	H *customised*	G *standardised*
■ capital is	J *required*	I *not required* *
■ before maturity	L *only reversal*	K *can close out*
■ instrument is	N *derivative*	N *derivative*
■ settles at	P *end of interest periods*	O *start of interest periods*

* This is true for banks but may not be true for some other types of institution.

3 Trading swaps

Dealing procedures

Dealing technology

The market in interest rate swaps is an *over-the-counter* or *OTC* market. Trading is conducted principally by telephone. Price information is disseminated over screen-based telecommunication networks operated by companies such as *Telerate* and *Reuters*. Financial information companies, such as *IFR* and *Thomson Financial Services,* and brokers contribute data and analysis to such networks. Brokers also provide price, other market information and transactions advice directly to their customers.

Deal details

In negotiating a swap, key financial details are agreed verbally between dealers. The list of these details is quite long and becomes even longer for non-generic swaps. A minimum list of the details which need to be agreed upfront in a swap deal are set out in a recommended checklist promulgated by the Bank of England in its *London Code of Conduct* and reproduced in *Box 3*. After a deal has been agreed verbally, key details are confirmed by an exchange of telexes or faxes, usually within 24 hours. Full contract documentation is agreed, signed and exchanged subsequently: thus, swaps are sometimes said to be dealt on an **as of** basis. However, a contract is generally assumed to exist on the basis of the initial verbal agreement between dealers, rather than the confirmations or the contract documentation (although this assumption may have legal weaknesses).

Box 3: The Bank of England's London Code of Conduct: suggested pre-deal checklist

Trade date
Customer name
       country of incorporation
       guarantee (if any)
Telex to
Telex number
Credit approved by

Customer pays: fixed/floating
Notional amount
Effective date
Maturity date
Currency
Trading desk
Firm
Counterparty

Fixed rate
Coupon rate
Coupon frequency
Day type
Non-business day roll convention
1st coupon payment due
1st coupon payment amount

Variable rate (1) customer pays/receives
Index
Spread
Coupon frequency
Reset frequency
Day type
Determination source
Rounding convention
Agent
Determination date convention
Non-business day roll convention
1st variable payment date
Gross initial/current variable rate

Variable rate (2) customer pays/receives
Index
Spread
Coupon frequency
Reset frequency
Day type
Determination source
Rounding convention

Agent
Determination date convention
Non-business day roll convention
1st reset date
1st variable/current payment date
Gross initial/current variable rate

Fees and collateral
Payment basis — gross/net
Premium/discount — they pay/we pay
       upfront amount
       paid by
       paid to
       account number
Broker name
       broker fee
Intermediary fee
Collateral
       letter of credit
       decline amount/year
       mark to market
Defer option
       defer rate
       defer benchmark
       benchmark spread
Asset information

Additional information

Salesperson
Trader

Source: Bank of England, London Code of Conduct

Negotiating price

In a coupon swap, the most important deal detail is the price of the swap (meaning the level of the fixed interest rate). If the swap is quoted in terms of a spread over a benchmark yield, dealers will agree the spread first, because this is the more volatile component, particularly for shorter-term swaps. They will then break off their negotiations to check whether they both have credit limits to deal with each other and whether there is enough room under the credit limits. If there are no credit constraints, the dealers will contact each other again and agree the level of the benchmark yield, which is added to the spread to fix the *all-in* swap rate. The benchmark yield is supposed to be fixed within a 'reasonable' (but undefined) period of agreeing the spread.

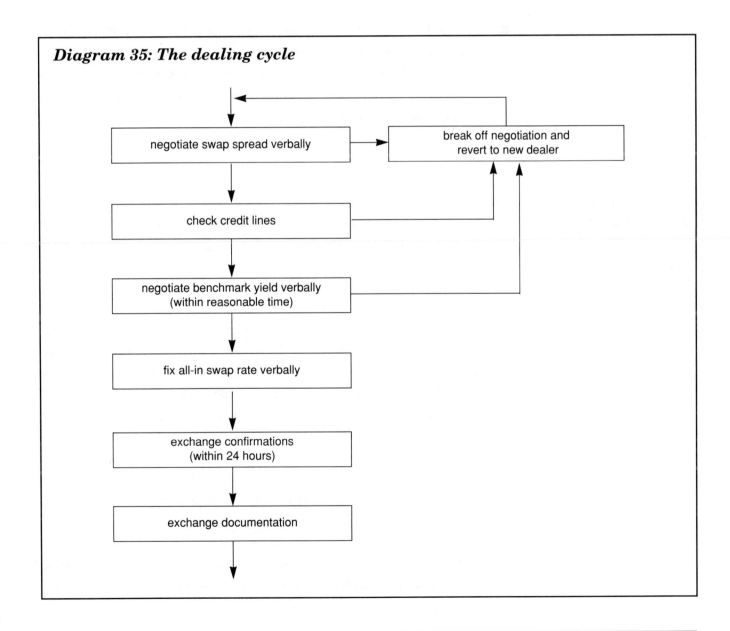

Diagram 35: The dealing cycle

Swap documentation

Coverage of swap documentation

A contract is *evidence* of the agreement of the counterparties to a specific transaction and provides a detailed *definition of* the transaction itself in respect of:

- *financial* terms and conditions of the transaction, meaning the rights which can be exercised and the obligations which must be performed by the counterparties: in other words, the details of the deal;

- *legal* framework for the contract, meaning rights in law of *enforcement* of the agreed financial terms and conditions in the event of problems such as default by a counterparty: this covers matters such as the definition of an *event of default,* methods of computing damages, governing law and so forth.

Moves to standardise documentation

Early swap trading was hampered by the complexity of documentation, which reflected the novelty of the instrument and the consequent need to provide adequate financial and legal definitions. One major issue was whether swaps were gaming contracts, as the latter are legally unenforceable. The need to establish swaps as instruments of commerce was particularly important in early transactions, when there was a lack of legal precedent and little custom and usage which the markets could offer to the courts. Contracts therefore contained extensive legal opinion in support of the commercial nature of swaps and, even on fairly straightforward transactions, could extend to 60 pages and take over three months to finalise. They were also expensive. Serious backlogs in documentation had developed in the swaps market by 1984. Other problems were:

- *liquidity* was constrained by cumbersome documentation procedures;

- documentation added to transactions *costs* and could not be sustained with dealing spreads under competitive pressure;

■ swaps usually commence before they are documented, so that subsequent failures to agree documentation meant counterparties suffered an *unexpected loss of protection* or *profit* by being deprived of either hedge, risk or arbitrage positions, which they had assumed to be in place;

■ lack of uniformity between contracts prevented the *netting* of payments due through different swaps which was needed to allow market-makers to make more efficient use of their credit lines;

■ lack of uniformity between contracts and the consequent lack of transparency obscured the overall *risk exposure* of swap counterparties and made it difficult to manage swaps within a portfolio;

■ lack of uniformity between contracts and the consequent lack of transparency obstructed attempts to trade swaps and develop a *secondary market*.

In order to overcome these problems, active swap counterparties have tried to standardise documentation: initially, on a *bilateral* basis with other active counterparties; and then, through *multilateral* efforts sponsored by market associations.

Bilateral documentation

Early market-makers agreed **master contracts** with active counterparties which permitted negotiations for most swaps to be limited to key details, with other terms and conditions agreed simply by reference to the master contract. Most master contracts covered interest rate swaps: a few covered currency swaps. Master agreements were often differentiated by type of counterparty, for example, into bank-bank and bank-corporate, as well as in terms of whether the counterparty was domestic or foreign.

Multilateral documentation	Bilateral master contracts helped but did not solve the delays in swap documentation, prompting various efforts to produce a market-wide standard for documentation which could be used by a wide range of counterparties for a wide range of swaps. The two principal initiatives have originated from:

■   British Bankers' Association (BBA);

■   International Swap Dealers' Association (ISDA).[1]

BBA documentation	In August 1985, the BBA promulgated its *BBAIRS Terms (Recommended Terms and Conditions for London Interbank Interest Rate Swaps)*. These allow the negotiation of swaps to be limited to agreement on key details, with reference to BBAIRS Terms covering other terms and conditions. BBAIRS Terms were intended to apply to swaps of less than two years' maturity, traded interbank in London and involving US dollars, sterling, Deutsche marks, Swiss francs or yen in (1) single-currency coupon swaps, (2) currency swaps[2] and cross-currency coupon swaps or (3) cross-currency basis swaps. The Terms provide definitions of financial terms and conditions, sample confirmations and provisions setting out rights of enforcement in the event of a default. A sample BBAIRS confirmation is reproduced in *Box 4*. In addition to documentation, BBAIRS Terms also provide conventions for conducting negotiations. The aim was to establish 'normal market practice' for London and the convention applied is that, unless otherwise stated, short-term swaps dealt in London are assumed to be subject to BBAIRS Terms.

BBAIRS Interest Settlement Rate	A practical step taken in the BBAIRS Terms was to define the Libor index to be used for periodically fixing the floating interest rate in swaps. To support this definition, the BBA arranged for *Telerate* to calculate and publish daily a list of **BBAIRS Interest Settlement Rates** for each monthly maturity between one **and 12 months for each of the 11 relevant** currencies: these are published on *Telerate* screen pages 3740–50. These rates are also used to settle FRA transactions under the BBA's *FRABBA Terms*. A copy of the page for sterling Libor is reproduced in Diagram 36.

Box 4: BBAIRS Terms — example of confirmation between swap counterparties

FIXED RATE PAYER BANK PLC,
Main Street
LONDON EC2

To: Floating Rate Payer Bank Inc   Date: 26 September 1985
             Moorgate   Our Ref: XYZ0001
             LONDON EC2

CONFIRMATION OF SINGLE CURRENCY FIXED/FLOATING INTEREST RATE SWAP AGREEMENT

We hereby confirm particulars in respect of the following single currency fixed/floating Interest Rate Swap Agreement entered between us subject to the British Bankers' Association's Recommended Terms and Conditions ("BBAIRS Terms") dated August 1985.

Contract Date:	26 September 1985
Fixed Rate Payer:	Fixed Rate Payer Bank PLC
Floating Rate Payer:	Floating Rate Payer Bank Inc
Direct/Broker:	Broker
Commencement Date:	28 September 1985
Maturity Date:	30 September 1986
Currency:	US dollars
Notional Principal:	US$20m
Fixed Rate Payments:	
Fixed Rate:	12.12500% per annum
Floating Rate:	First period *11.50000%* thereafter <u>three</u> months BBAIRS Settlement Rate
Fixed Rate Payment Dates:	Maturity Date
Floating Rate Payment Dates:	19/12/85 — 20/03/86 — 19/06/86 — 30/09/86
Variation to BBAIRS Terms:	None
Fixed Rate Payers Account:	ABC Bank, New York
Floating Rate Payers Account:	XYZ Bank, New York

PLEASE TELEPHONE OR CABLE US IMMEDIATELY SHOULD THE PARTICULARS OF THIS CONFIRMATION NOT BE IN ACCORDANCE WITH YOUR UNDERSTANDING

For   _____

    _____

   (title)

Source: BBA

Diagram 36: BBA Interest Settlement Rates

[BRITISH BANKERS ASSOC INTEREST SETTLEMENT RATES]					PG 3740

[PG 3745] FOR INDEX OF REFERENCE BANKS, RECAPS & BBA DEFINITIONS
RATES AT 11:00 LONDON TIME 02/NOV/92   [OTHER LIBORS–3750]

	[FIXED]	[FIXED]	[FIXED]	[FIXED]	[FIXED]	[FIXED]
CCY	AUD	FRF	CAD	ITL	ESP	NGL
1MO	5.76563	9.68750	7.37500	15.00000	14.01563	9.00000
2MO	5.87500	9.68750	6.50000	14.87500	13.92188	9.00000
3MO	5.93750	9.75000	6.12500	14.62500	13.87500	8.87500
4MO	5.98438	9.68750	5.96875	14.40625	13.85938	8.75000
5MO	6.01563	9.56250	5.85938	14.18750	13.81250	8.62500
6MO	6.06250	9.50000	5.75000	13.96875	13.79688	8.56250
7MO	6.12500	9.37500	5.75000	13.87500	13.76563	8.43750

[BRITISH BANKERS ASSOC INTEREST SETTLEMENT RATES]					PG 3750

[PG 3745] FOR INDEX OF REFERENCE BANKS, RECAPS & BBA DEFINITIONS
RATES AT 11:00 LONDON TIME 02/NOV/92   [OTHER LIBORS–3740]

	[FIXED]	[FIXED]	[FIXED]	[FIXED]	[FIXED]	[FIXED]
CCY	USD	GBP	DEM	CHF	JPY	ECU
1MO	3.25000	8.18750	9.12500	6.39063	3.93750	10.56250
2MO	3.62500	7.87500	9.06250	6.50000	3.87500	10.50000
3MO	3.62500	7.62500	9.00000	6.43750	3.79688	10.37500
4MO	3.62500	7.39063	8.85938	6.37500	3.75000	10.12500
5MO	3.62500	7.23438	8.72656	6.32813	3.75000	9.97656
6MO	3.62500	7.06250	8.62500	6.32813	3.75000	9.83594
7MO	3.65625	7.01563	8.50000	6.25000	3.75000	9.69531

BBAIRS Terms have proved a successful initiative. Their relative simplicity appealed to dealers and they performed well within the cohesive London market. The Terms were widely adopted as a model in other centres, for example, providing the basis for the *AIRS Terms* in Australia[3], and were also adapted by some counterparties for swaps beyond two years' maturity. However, the BBAIRS Terms solved only part of the documentation problem and have now largely been superseded by the more comprehensive attempt at standardisation undertaken by ISDA.

ISDA documentation

In June 1985, ISDA published a *Code of Standard Wording, Assumptions and Provisions for Swaps* (the *ISDA Swaps Code*). This was a menu from which counterparties could draw when drafting a contract for US dollar swaps. The Code dealt mainly with financial terms and conditions, such as calculation of interest and termination payments. It was revised and expanded in 1986, to address rights of enforcement and credit provisions.

In 1987, ISDA published two master contracts for:

■ US dollar interest rate swaps — the *Interest Rate Swap Agreement (the Rate Swap Master* agreement);

■ interest rate and currency swaps in or between a variety of currencies[4] — the *Interest Rate and Currency Exchange Agreement (the Rate and Currency Swap Master* agreement).

The dollar contract was based on the ISDA Swap Code and the non-dollar contract on a supplement to the Code, the *1987 Interest Rate and Currency Exchange Definitions*. The former is limited to State of New York law: but the latter is also available under English law.

Each ISDA master contract is divided into two parts:

■ Basic terms and conditions.

■ A *Schedule* on which to complete, supplement or modify the basic terms and conditions. The Schedule includes a residual *Other Provisions* category to which credit provisions can be added (eg, special cross-default clauses, covenants and credit support such as guarantees and collateral). ISDA has issued a *User's Guide* to assist the customisation of the Schedule.

An ISDA master contract, once in place between two counterparties, absorbs all subsequent swaps between them. The details of new swaps are added to the master contract as appendices. Each time a new swap is added, a new contract is created assuming all outstanding deals (a process called **novation**). The fact that all swaps are subsumed within a single contract significantly facilitates netting and portfolio management of swaps. Of course, use of a master contract only makes sense with active counterparties and therefore tends to be limited to interbank relationships.

The primary market: banks

Arrangers

Early intermediaries tried to avoid taking risk in the swap market by acting as arrangers of swap deals between end-users. Arrangers do not intermediate the interest payments through swaps, but simply act as *agents* and accordingly charge flat *fees* (up to 1/2%). The corporate finance role of new issue arbitrage was reflected in the dominance of the early swap market by *merchant* and *investment banks*.

Matched-book dealers

As more diverse end-users entered the market, it became necessary for intermediary banks to act as *principals* in swaps. There were a number of reasons. End-users often looked for anonymity. Many could not undertake their own credit analysis and therefore proved reluctant to accept credit risk on non-banks. The exposure to credit risk involved in acting as a principal intermediary encouraged *commercial banks* to enter the swap market. Commercial banks tend to be ready to deal with a wider variety of counterparties than other financial institutions, as they typically have the capability to analyse credit risk and the balance sheet to accommodate it. Notwithstanding their own credit problems, commercial banks are generally preferred to non-bank names, which may not be acceptable at all to other non-banks[5]. In turn, commercial banks have been attracted by the role which swaps could play in supporting, through new issue arbitrage, the securities businesses which they have been establishing. The off-balance sheet nature of swaps has also been an attractive source of profits for banks with balance sheets impaired by sovereign and other debt problems.

Principal intermediaries initially limited themselves to running **matched books**, meaning that they only transacted a swap if there was a more or less equal and opposite swap immediately available as a hedge. Finding such matching or **reverse** swaps could take three months, depending on the currency and the complexity of the particular swap. To cover their exposure to the credit risk of the end-user counterparties, intermediary banks charged risk-related dealing spreads in the form of differences between the fixed interest rate paid to one end-user and that received from the other end-user (making a net percentage return per annum rather than the one-off percentage represented by a flat fee). Arrangement fees persisted for a time as a charge for the documentation and design of swaps, but have been made increasingly rare by competition, other than for complex swap structures involving financial engineering.

Market-makers

While swaps originated for the purpose of new issue arbitrage, they have become more and more a tool of asset liability management. The more active and continuous nature of this function has required a more liquid market in interest rate swaps. This liquidity was provided in the major currencies through the emergence of intermediaries willing to *make markets*, meaning continuously quoting two-way prices at which they stand ready to deal in 'reasonable' amounts in most trading conditions and without immediately available matched swaps. Most market-makers still aim to run matched books in swaps, but will accept temporary exposure to the risk on unmatched swap positions. This willingness reflects the development of techniques for:

- temporarily hedging or **warehousing** individual swaps before matching swaps become available (temporary can mean three months for complex swaps in minor currencies);

- **portfolio management** of the overall risk on swap books.

Market-making is dominated by the commercial banks for the same reasons of credit risk which allow that type of institution to dominate as swap principals.

Assignment brokering

Competition in the swap market has so narrowed dealing spreads that many market-makers, particularly institutions with relatively small balance sheets and limited capital, such as merchant and investment banks, have tried to avoid building up large swap books and exposures to credit risk by selling or **assigning** swaps from their own swap books. Such assignment brokering is not brokering in the strict sense of acting like an agent, as swaps cross the balance sheet. Assignment brokering has been facilitated by the standardisation of swap documentation and the wider inclusion of assignment clauses in swap contracts. Given the reduction in credit risk exposure which is achieved by assignment brokering, dealing spreads are narrower than for running a swap book.

Table 8: Comparison of swap intermediation

Intermediary role	Type of intermediary	Return	Risk
arranger	merchant bank investment bank	arrangement fee	no risk
matched-book dealer	commercial bank	arrangement fee and dealing spread	permanent credit risk but no market risk
market-maker	commercial bank	dealing spread	permanent credit risk and temporary market risk
assignment broker	merchant bank investment bank	dealing spread	temporary credit risk and temporary market risk

Warehousing term swaps

Hedging techniques were developed initially for *term swaps*. It was explained in *Part One* that interest rate swaps are the off-balance sheet equivalent of gap positions opened up on the balance sheet using cash instruments. Cash securities can therefore be used to hedge swaps. The problem is that hedge instruments need to be (1) liquid, so that they are cheap and easy to put on and take off, and (2) preferably free of credit risk, so that hedges do not collapse. The only cash bonds which are sufficiently liquid and also default-free are government bonds.

An example

Take the example of a payer of fixed interest through a coupon swap, who is exposed to the risk of a fall in interest rates (which will reduce floating interest received through the swap, while payments are fixed). To put a hedge on this swap, it is necessary to buy government bonds. Any subsequent fall in interest rates, which reduces the profitability of the swap, will increase the price of the bonds. If the swap and the bond have the same maturity, the capital gain on the bonds should more or less equal the income loss on the swap[6].

The purchase of bonds also has to be financed. As the hedge is temporary and for an unknown period, it is usual to fund it with overnight money. In the US dollar swap market, funding is often raised through overnight *repos* (sale-and-repurchase agreements). The bonds which have been purchased as the hedge are lent out in return for cash, subject to an agreement that they will be returned at an agreed date. The lender of the securities and receiver of the cash also pays interest — at the *repo rate* — to the other counterparty. The repo proceeds are used to pay for the bonds (this is all possible as the necessary payments and deliveries are all settled at close of business). In the sterling swap market, financing is usually raised by straightforward overnight borrowing in the money market. The cost of funding the bonds will be offset, at least partly, by the floating interest received through the swap. However, overnight interest rates are repriced each day, whereas the floating interest received through the swap is usually six-month Libor. This gives rise to basis risk. With a positive yield curve, six-month Libor exceeds overnight interest rates and the floating side of the hedge would be profitable. With a negative yield curve, there would be a loss. This type of hedge is illustrated in Diagram 37. A worked example of warehousing a US dollar swap is set out in *Case Study II*.

Case Study II: Warehousing a US dollar interest rate swap

A swap market-maker quotes 60–65 for five-year US dollar coupon swaps (meaning 60–65 basis points over the yield on the on-the-run US Treasury note with the closest tenor). The floating interest rate is six-month US dollar Libor. The yield on the on-the-run five-year US Treasury note (coupon 8%, trading at 100.5085) is 7.875% per annum; six-month Libor is 7.375% per annum. The overnight repo rate is 6.680% per annum.

A customer transacts a five-year swap with a notional principal amount of US$10m in which it receives and the market-maker pays fixed interest: the fixed interest is therefore fixed at 60 basis points over the yield on the on-the-run five-year US Treasury note, which gives an all-in rate of 7.875% + 60 basis points = 8.475% per annum.

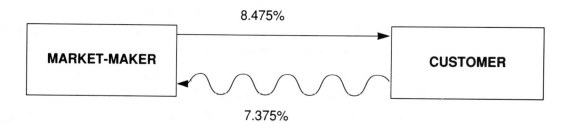

8.475%

MARKET-MAKER → CUSTOMER

7.375%

The market-maker runs a matched swap book. It therefore looks for a matching swap in which it will receive fixed interest. Until it finds such a match, it is exposed to the risk of an interest rate fall: this would reduce the fixed interest rate on new swaps and may mean that a matching swap will pay it less fixed interest than it is paying out through the swap it is seeking to match.

Assume that the market-maker is, in fact, unable to find a matching swap before close of business. It therefore hedges its interest rate exposure by warehousing the swap: it buys US$10m of the on-the-run five-year US Treasury note. It funds the purchase of the notes with the proceeds from an overnight repo: it lends the notes overnight in exchange for cash, on which it pays the overnight repo rate, subject to an agreement to have the notes returned the following day and to repay the cash in exchange. The cost of warehousing the swap is shown in the following table. Note that the hedge yields a small profit. The cost of the hedge should also include the transactions costs of buying and selling US Treasury notes: unless the swap market-maker is also a market-maker in US Treasury securities, it is likely to lose the dealing spread each time (by buying the securities at some other institution's selling price and selling at some other institution's buying price). In practice, the dealing spread is likely to be about a 1/32nd and the cost on each leg of the hedge will be 1/32 x US$10,000,000 = US$3,125.

Market-maker

	swap	hedge
fixed interest	−8.475	
floating interest	+7.375	
bond yield	+7.875	
overnight repo rate	−6.680	
sub-totals	−1.100	+1.195p
total	+0.095	

Assume interest rates fall the next day, before a matching swap can be transacted, with yields on the on-the-run five-year US Treasury falling to 7.625%. Assume also that spreads do not change on five-year swaps and remain at 60–65. If the market-maker now manages to transact a matching swap, it will receive fixed interest at 65 basis points over Treasury yields, which gives an all-in rate of 7.625% + 65 basis points = 8.275% per annum. This means it will make a loss of 8.275% – 8.475% = 20 basis points per annum.

Over the five years of the swap, a loss of 20 basis points per annum on a notional principal amount of US$10m US$100,000 which has a net present value (discounted at the new swap rate) of US$79,279.

The loss on the matched swap is, however, offset by the increase in the price of the US Treasury notes following the fall in interest rates. A fall in the yield on five-year US Treasury notes with a coupon of 8% from 7.875% to 7.625% produces a rise in price from 79,279 to 101.535088, generating a capital gain of 1.026588 x US$10m = US$102,659. This offsets the loss of US$80,557 (in net present value terms) to leave a residual profit of US$23,380. The residual profit is due to the fact that, although the yield on US Treasury notes fell by 25 basis points, the market-maker retrieved 5 basis points by being able to maintain swap spreads at 60–65. Without this 5 basis points, the loss on the matching swap would have been 25 basis points, which would have amounted to US$125,000 which has a net present value of US$99,098 — almost exactly the same as the capital gain on the US Treasury notes of US$102,659.

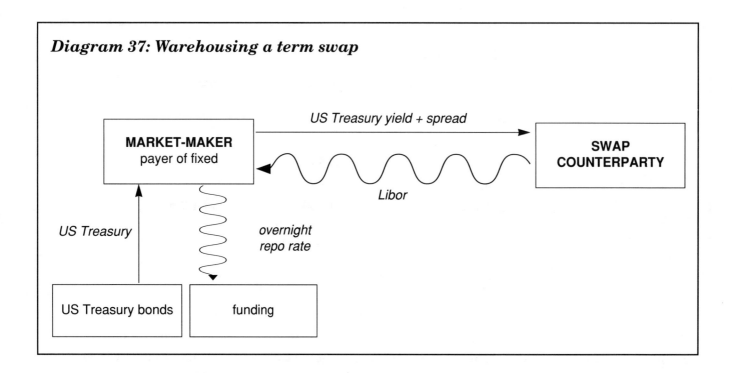

Diagram 37: Warehousing a term swap

The receiver of fixed interest through a coupon swap would hedge by borrowing the appropriate bonds, then selling them to establish a short position. The proceeds from this sale would be used to fund the borrowing. In the US dollar swap market, bonds would be borrowed through a *reverse repo* (reverse sale-and-repurchase agreement), in which the bonds are borrowed, in return for cash, subject to an agreement to return them at an agreed date. In the sterling swap market, only gilt-edged market-makers and discount houses can go short of gilt-edged securities, so other institutions would have to use gilt futures to go short. The return on the proceeds from selling bonds offsets, at least partly, the floating interest paid through the swap. This type of hedge is illustrated in Diagram 38 below.

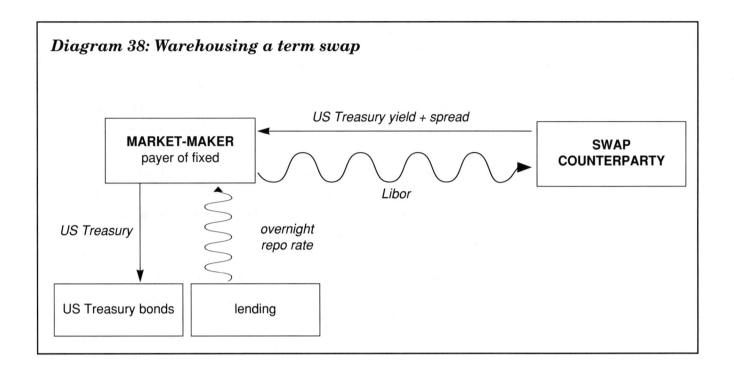

Diagram 38: Warehousing a term swap

Warehousing term swaps with futures

Instead of using cash government bonds, the fixed interest stream in a coupon swap can be hedged with *futures* contracts on government bonds and the floating interest stream can be hedged with short-term interest rate futures contracts. As derivative instruments, which require no payments of principal, futures should provide a more efficient hedge than cash bonds. The problem is that bond futures tend to be based on notional bonds with long tenors, eg, at least 10 years in the long gilt future on Liffe and at least 15 years in the US T-bond contract on CBOT. Swap maturities, on the other hand, are rarely beyond 10 years, which means that there is likely to be considerable basis risk in hedging fixed interest streams with bond futures. There is less (although still significant) basis risk in using short-term interest rate futures to hedge floating interest counterstreams: typically, this would involve three-month interest rate futures against six-month Libor in swaps. As with other sources of basis risk, some market-makers accept and manage such positions.

Spread risk

It was noted in *Part One* that swaps in certain major currencies such as US dollar and sterling are quoted in terms of *swap spreads*[7] over *benchmark* interest rates, where the benchmark interest rates are usually yields on the most liquid government bonds with appropriate tenors. The technique of warehousing term swaps with government bonds covers most of the risk on an unmatched swap, but leaves an exposure to change in the *spread* over the government bond yield[8]. This residual exposure is called **swap spread risk** and can be a very serious problem as spreads are usually very volatile, particularly for shorter-term swaps. Take the example of a warehousing operation illustrated in Diagram 38 above, in which the receiver of fixed interest through a coupon swap hedges by selling government bonds. The swap spread risk is that spreads over government bond yields will widen. If this occurs, and government bond yields do not fall, matching swaps to reverse the existing swap will involve paying out at a higher fixed interest rate than is being received from the existing swap, without any offset from the hedge.

A major example of spread risk was provided in 1987, when Citibank announced bad debt provisions of some $3bn. This announcement severely dented confidence in other US money centre banks with exposure to sovereign debt by highlighting the seriousness of the problem and posing a question as to whether others had the wherewithal to follow Citibank's lead. The issue was reflected in a sudden widening of spreads over US Treasury bond yields in the cash bond and interest rate swap markets. Treasury yields hardly flinched, so fixed interest rates on swaps rose by the amount of the rise in the swap spread. Swap market-makers who were net receivers of fixed interest, and who had therefore warehoused by selling US Treasuries, found themselves facing serious swap spread losses, as they had to pay higher fixed rates on matching swaps without compensation from their hedges.

Buying and selling

Because spread risk cannot be hedged, other than by reverse swaps, the swap market is said to be a market in swap spreads. A payer of fixed interest through a coupon swap is said to *buy* or *go long* of the spread, and benefits when spreads widen or *go out*, because a subsequent reversal swap, through which fixed interest is received, would be at a higher fixed rate (assuming the benchmark yield did not fall). On the other hand, a receiver of fixed interest through a swap is said to *sell* or *go short* of the spread and benefits when spreads narrow or *come in*, because a subsequent reversal swap, through which fixed interest is paid, would be at a lower fixed rate (again assuming the benchmark yield did not fall). In practice, swaps tend to be used to take spread positions rather than absolute interest rate positions. Other markets, such as those in government bonds and futures, offer better liquidity in absolute interest rates.

The behaviour of spreads

Swap spreads reflect supply and demand for swaps, but the benchmark yield is unlikely to be affected by the supply and demand for swaps, given the relative size and liquidity of the markets in the bonds typically used to provide benchmark yields. The arbitrage opportunities against cash or derivative instruments and the volume of new bond issues to be swapped into synthetic FRNs are important factors in the supply and demand of swaps. For example, a surge in new issues will be reflected in increased demand for swaps paying fixed interest in order to arbitrage against bond yields: demand to receive fixed interest will allow payers of fixed interest to reduce swap spreads. The general direction of interest rates is another important factor in determining swap spread, as noted in *Part Two,* government bond yields change faster than yields in other bond markets so that a rise in general interest rates will narrow swap spreads; and vice versa.

Spread curves

Given that swap spreads represent the trading price for term swaps, market-makers will seek to build up a familiarity with the behaviour of spreads. A basic analytical tool is a chart, similar to a yield curve, plotting the spreads prevailing currently across a range of maturities. This is the **spread curve** or term structure of swap spreads.

In addition to monitoring the behaviour of the current spread curve across a range of maturities (a *cross-sectional* analysis), market-makers will also analyse the historical behaviour of the spreads for particular maturities over time (a *time series* analysis).

Warehousing money market swaps

Considerable liquidity has developed in many currencies in the one and two-year *money market swaps*. The development of money market swaps has mirrored the growing availability of short-term interest rate futures and FRAs with which to hedge and against which to arbitrage. Money market swaps are warehoused with *strips* of futures or sometimes FRAs. The principle of stripping futures and FRAs is explained in *Part Two* and the arithmetic is demonstrated in *Part Four*. Because money market swaps are so closely connected with futures, their behaviour is very sensitive to arbitrage opportunities and consequently more volatile than term swaps, where demand for new issues arbitrage plays an important and measured role.

Risk tolerance

While the development of warehousing techniques has been primarily responsible for enabling market-making in swaps, it has also reflected the fact that swap intermediaries have become more familiar with the risks associated with swaps and more confident of their ability to manage risk positions. Swap risks have been recognised as being equivalent to those generated by conventional cash instruments. Greater confidence about swap risks means that market-makers sometimes do not warehouse their swaps and frequently absorb the basis risk arising from mismatches between swaps, or even aggressively run positions in the basis risk. Such mismatches may be between notional principal amounts, maturities, interest payment dates, floating interest rate reset dates and indexes, and so forth. In part, willingness to absorb hedging mismatches reflects the attraction of wider dealing spreads in return for taking the extra risk. Ultimately, however, such flexibility is a practical requirement of market-making. There is a trade-off between the precision and practicality of hedging. Market-makers need to accept mismatching, if they are going to be able to transact any volume of swaps.

Portfolio management of swaps

The matching and warehousing of individual swaps has a number of drawbacks for market-makers and has encouraged the development of a *pooling* rather than a *pairing* approach to managing swap books which involves their aggregation into portfolios. The incentives are:

■ mismatches are not easy to hedge by individual matching (particularly mismatches between reset dates on floating interest rates and between floating interest rate indexes): pooling can offer greater opportunities to offset this through *diversification*[9];

■ the increase in the *volume* and *speed* of turnover in swaps, as they have shifted from being primarily an instrument of corporate finance to one of asset and liability management, has made their individual matching impractical and administratively too costly: portfolio management of swaps requires less hedging activity because the internal offsetting of mismatches reduces total risk;

■ recognition that the risks generated by swaps are analagous to those on conventional cash instruments has encouraged the *integration* of swap book management with general asset and liability management, using the risk or arbitrage positions taken through the balance sheet to hedge swaps and vice versa.

■ it is difficult to match *complex swaps* individually: within a portfolio, however, there is more opportunity to hedge the various features of a complex structure separately.

Building a portfolio

The integration of interest rate swaps into a portfolio depends on the *unbundling* or breaking up of each swap into individual cash flows which are simple enough to be compared and offset against each other and the cash flows from other swaps (as well as other types of instrument). This process is illustrated in Diagram 39 below.

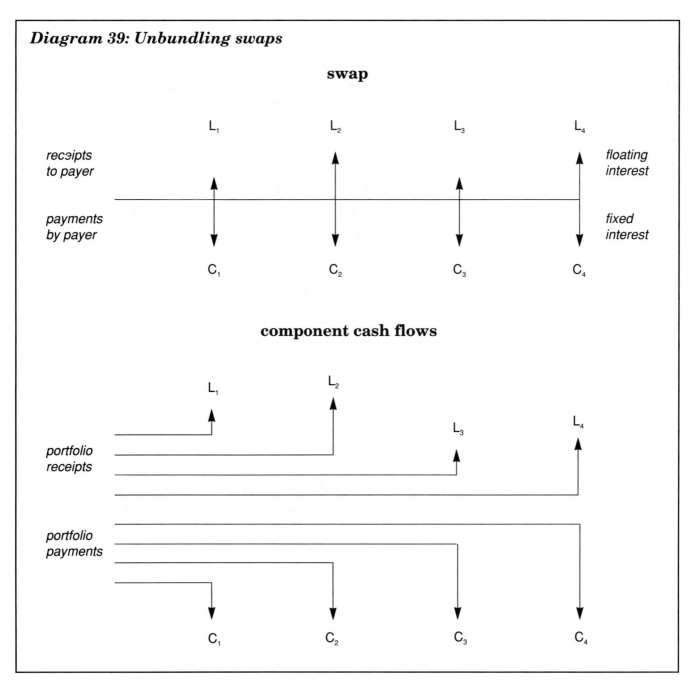

Diagram 39: Unbundling swaps

Before individual cash flows are offset against each other, they are adjusted for the time value of money by discounting to *present value*. Discount rates are taken from the yield curves of relevant floating interest rate indexes (usually ignoring the bid-offer spread). By netting out the present value of individual cash flows, a *residual risk exposure* is left, which should be much smaller than the exposure on a swap book in which transactions are individually warehoused and matched. Any hedging is limited to this residual.

Organising a portfolio

Before netting out cash flows, there is a *segregation* of fixed from floating interest. The two types of interest behave differently and are hedged using different instruments. Fixed interest behaves like fixed-income bonds and is normally hedged with government bonds; floating interest behaves like short-term money market securities and is normally hedged with these instruments or, more usually, with matching swaps, basis swaps or derivatives. Floating interest flows may be further *sub-divided* in terms of the different floating-rate indexes. It is also usual to disaggregate interest flows into discrete periods, rather than analyse them on a daily basis (except where there are large exposures or concentrations of exposures on particular repricing dates). The result is a schedule with the same format as a traditional interest rate mismatch ladder or gap report.

Valuation of future floating interest flows

A key problem in building a swap portfolio is that future floating interest rates are unknown. The usual solution is to use implied *forward-forward interest rates* calculated from current yield curves. The arithmetic for valuing future floating interest with implied forward-foward rates is explained in *Part Four* on *Pricing and Valuing Swaps*.

The behaviour of portfolios

If fixed interest receipts are systematically repriced before fixed interest payments, there will be a gain if interest rates rise and a loss if rates fall. The sensitivity of the overall floating interest rate portfolio (which aggregates the floating-rate sub-portfolios) depends on:

■ the change in the shape of the yield curve for each relevant floating-rate index;

■ the relative changes in the shapes of the yield curves for the relevant floating-rate indexes, in other words, changes in spreads;

■ the average maturity of interest receipts relative to the average maturity of interest payments.

For example, if floating interest receipts were priced off three-month Libor and floating interest payments off a 30-day commercial paper index, a steepening of the yield curve would tend to produce a portfolio gain. Floating-rate portfolios tend to be volatile and very sensitive to the addition of new swaps and the repricing of existing swaps.

Managing fixed interest cash flows

The exposure on fixed interest flows in swap portfolios has attracted most attention from risk managers on the grounds that such longer-term interest rates represent a longer-term exposure and are inherently riskier than the shorter-term rates used on the floating side of swaps. After offsetting opposing fixed interest flows, residual interest rate exposure can be hedged (by putting on matching swaps or hedging with different instruments) or the position can be run. Even if the position is hedged, there is likely to be basis risk arising from mismatches or the inefficiency of the hedge.

Managing floating interest cash flows

The exposure on the floating interest flows in swap portfolios usually attracts less attention than that on fixed interest flows because the regular resetting of floating interest rates in swaps (usually every six months at least) means the floating interest rates on receipts and payments through swaps booked at different times should not diverge to the same degree as the fixed interest rates on receipts and payments through swaps booked at different times. However, experience has shown that even minor mismatches between floating interest receipts and payments (eg, differences in indexes, interest payment dates and floating interest rate reset dates) represent serious exposures. The volatility of floating interest portfolios has encouraged the application of sophisticated statistical methods to estimate exposure. There are a number of approaches to managing floating rate risk:

■   a portfolio approach to automatically and passively reduce net exposure through diversification;

■   additional diversification by integrating floating interest portfolios with cash portfolios;

■   more active hedging of net floating rate risk by hedging with

   — matching swaps
   — basis swaps
   — derivatives
   — money market securities;

■   a position can be run with the net floating-rate risk.

Some institutions manage their floating interest portfolios on a break-even basis and only actively seek profits on their fixed interest portfolios.

The primary market: brokers

The role of brokers

Dealers can trade interest rate swaps through *brokers*, who act as agents, arranging deals by matching swap counterparties, but not actually participating in transactions themselves. Unlike dealers, who seek to earn a dealing spread, but similar to arrangers, brokers are paid flat fees or *brokerage* commissions which are related to the size of a deal (in terms of its notional principal amount) rather than its price. This form of remuneration is intended to ensure that brokers are solely interested in arranging deals and therefore in securing mutually attractive prices for counterparties. Typical brokerage rates for swaps, before volume-related discounts, are a flat 1 basis point from each counterparty. Brokerage is paid upfront.

Broking swaps

A broker continuously takes prices from customers, and then selects and broadcasts the cheapest selling price and the most generous buying price to have been quoted for each maturity of the swap. The series of two-way prices for a range of maturities which a broker broadcasts back to customers is called a **broker's run**. If a customer *hits* one of these prices, the broker passes the identity of the customer who originated the price and vice versa. For this reason, swaps brokers are often called **name-passing brokers**.

Brokers' information screens

Brokers disseminate swap prices over information networks such as *Telerate* and *Reuters*. The prices posted on screens are *indicative* only, and a dealer would need to contact the broker directly in order to secure *firm* dealing prices. A typical broker's screen is reproduced in Diagram 40 over the page.

Diagram 40: Broker's swap screen

US DOLLAR INTEREST RATE SWAP			ANN FIXED VS USD LIBOR –ACT/360–	CLOSING RATES	
				STERLING	– ICAQ
					– ICAO
MATURITY		SPREAD		DM/SF/ECU/NLG	– ICAR
2 YRS	1094+	35–31	4.81–4.77	LIRE/SPAIN	– ICAS
3 YRS	0895+	52–48	5.46–5.42	YN/FFR/BF/NLG	– ICAT
4 YRS	INTRP	49–45	5.96–5.92	DMCAPS/FLOORS– ICAU
5 YRS	1097+	38–34	6.32–6.28	BASIS SWAPS	– ICAY
7 YRS	1099+	41–37	6.85–6.81	LDC DEBT	– QAQA
10 YRS	0802+	42–38	7.29–7.25	OIL SWAPS	– ICAS
STERLING INTEREST RATE SWAPS		GILT	SEMI-ANN SPREAD	A-365F	
2 YRS	6.78–6.74	9 94			
3 YRS	7.10–7.06	10Q 95			
4 YRS	7.36–7.31	10 96			
5 YRS	7.57–7.53	8T 97			
7 YRS	8.00–7.96	9 00			
10 YRS	8.42–8.36	9T 02			

Sources: Reuters; Intercapital Brokers

Advisory services

Brokers do not just recycle swap prices and match customers. They also:

■ provide information on the state of the market, based on their unique perspective (this is a requirement for authorisation to operate as a broker in London);

■ broke transactions complementary to swaps being brokered, eg, where the counterparties to a brokered coupon swap are both seeking to warehouse their sides of that swap, the broker can arrange for the payer of fixed interest through the swap to buy government bonds from the seller of fixed interest;

■ offer technical assistance to customers, such as suggestions for structuring profitable transactions, including arbitrages (the more deals involved, the more brokerage).

The secondary market: termination and assignment

What is termination?

Instead of reversing swaps, they can be cancelled. This process of **termination** requires the agreement of both counterparties, which may be an obstacle. Termination has the advantage over reversal of reducing exposure to credit risk.

What is assignment?

Instead of reversing or terminating swaps, it is possible to sell or **assign** them to new counterparties[10]. In other words, a buyer (the *assignee*) substitutes for one of the original counterparties (the *assignor*). For reasons of credit risk, assignment requires that the remaining counterparty approves the assignee. In recent years, assignment has been by **novation**, meaning that the swap contract to be assigned is in fact terminated and a new identical contract created between the remaining counterparty and the assignee. The assigning of swaps has created a nascent *secondary market*. One estimate puts the secondary market at about 20–25% of the total swaps turnover. However, the level of activity in the secondary swap market is constrained by the need to transfer credit risk.

Termination or assignment valuation

When a swap is terminated or assigned, it is valued and a cash payment made between the buyer and the seller to compensate whoever is calculated to receive net future interest through the swap over the remainder of its life. Termination or assignment are therefore ways of immediately realising the value of a swap and recognising it as income in the current period (usually for tax reasons), whereas a swap reversal amortises this gain over the remaining life of the swaps. The valuation of swaps is discussed in *Part Four* on *Pricing and Valuing Swaps*.

Assignability in contracts

Assignment has been facilitated by the emergence of standardised swap documentation, which makes swaps more transparent and transferable. Newer swap documentation also tends to include, as a matter of course, an 'assignment clause' which allows either counterparty to assign its participation. The rights of the remaining party to refuse assignment are sometimes circumscribed by a statement to the effect that agreement may not be reasonably withheld. In practice, however, such ambiguous rights have had little practical effect.

Clearing house proposals

There are proposals being studied by ISDA for a swap clearing house, which would function like a futures and options exchange, trading highly-standardised swaps, with the clearing house intervening as a counterparty to all transactions and operating a margining system. In effect, such a clearing house would involve multilateral netting and would transform the credit risk on swaps. It would also make swaps freely-assignable. However, the proposal is a radical one and seems unlikely to be implemented in the foreseeable future.

Notes

1. ISDA was formed, in March 1985, around the informal group of bank representatives which was established in New York in 1984 to work on the standardisation of swap documentation.

2. 'Currency swap' is a term used to describe a cross-currency swap involving an exchange of two fixed interest streams, whereas 'cross-currency swap' describes a cross-currency swap between either fixed and floating interest streams (a coupon swap) or two floating interest streams (a basis swap).

3. Australian Financial Markets Association's General Terms and Conditions for Australian Dollar Fixed and Floating Interest Rate Swaps.

4. 14 currencies: Belgian franc, Canadian dollar, Deutsche mark, Dutch guilder, Ecu, French franc, Hong Kong dollar, Italian lira, Luxembourg franc, New Zealand dollar, sterling, US dollar and yen.

5. In the UK, there are also tax reasons: interest payments through a swap are subject to withholding tax, unless one of the counterparties is a bank.

6. It is necessary to take into account the transactions cost of putting on the hedge in the form of the dealing spread paid on the bonds. Assuming the hedger *takes* rather than makes prices in US Treasury securities, the bonds are bought at the quoting dealer's *selling* price and sold at the quoting dealer's *buying* price, thereby losing the intervening dealing spread.

7. Distinguish swap spreads from dealing spread. The former is the margin over the benchmark yield, which together constitute a swap price, whereas the latter is the differential between two swap prices, specifically the buying and the selling prices. The swap spread largely reflects credit risk; the dealing spread largely reflects market or price risk.

8. In terms of historical sequence, the convention of quoting the spread over a benchmark yield for term swaps actually derives from the use of government bonds in warehousing, even though swaps had been invented for use in new issue arbitrage against Eurobonds, which were already quoted this way. The use of bonds was pioneered after bond futures had exhibited unacceptable basis risk.

9. The sort of risk being diversified is known by investment managers as 'unsystematic' risk: risk which is specific to particular investments and so varies between them, allowing some offsetting when diverse investments are combined within a portfolio.

10. Assignments are sometimes called *buy-outs* or *sales.*

Self-Study Exercises: <u>Questions</u>   Part 3

Question 3.1:   What is the sequence of actions in a typical swap deal? Number the following list of actions in order: not all actions in the list are part of a typical swap deal.

    A   exchange documentation

    B   check credit lines

    C   agree benchmark yield

    D   confirmation by fax or telex

    E   agree swap spread

Question 3.2:   At what stage in the sequence selected in Question 3.1 above does a contract exist?

Question 3.3:   What is a swap *master contract*?

Question 3.4:   What is the *BBAIRS Settlement Rate*? Where are BBAIRS Settlement Rates published?

Question 3.5:   Match the definitions listed in the right-hand column to the types of swap intermediary listed in the left-hand column.

    A arranger   I arrange swap between two end-users without participating

    B market-maker   II selling swaps in which one is a counterparty to third parties

    C assignment broker   III commitment to quote two-way prices and deal at those prices

    D broker   IV intermediate as principal between two matching end-users

Question 3.6:   A bank has transacted a term US dollar coupon swap in which it pays fixed interest. It wishes to warehouse the swap. What are the instruments typically used to warehouse US dollar swaps?

Question 3.7: What are the interest rate risks to which the bank in Question 3.6 above remains exposed, despite having warehoused its swap?

Question 3.8: What is the only practical way of hedging swap spreads?

Question 3.9: Has the payer of fixed interest through a coupon swap bought or sold the swap spread? Will the payer of fixed interest gain or lose if the spread narrows?

Question 3.10: What are the techniques which are available to close out a swap position? Outline what each involves.

Self-Study Exercises: <u>Answers</u> Part 3

Answer 3.1:   The sequence of actions in a typical swap deal is:

1   E   agree swap spread

2   B   check credit lines

3   C   agree benchmark yield

4   D   confirmation by fax or telex

5   A   exchange documentation

Answer 3.2:   A contract is generally assumed to exist on the basis of the initial verbal agreement between dealers once the benchmark yield has been agreed (stage 3 in the sequence above) and an *all-in* swap rate fixed. This is before an exchange of confirmations or documentation. However, this point has never been legally tested.

Answer 3.3:   A swap *master contract* is a standard form of contract which counterparties amend for each new deal, usually only in respect of key details which are specific to the new transaction, such as price, maturity, notional principal amount, etc. This allows market-makers in particular to limit deal negotiations to key details, with other terms and conditions agreed simply by reference to the master contract. The ISDA master contracts work by novation: each new deal is added as an appendix to the master contract and becomes part of a single integrated contract together with all previous deals under the master contract.

Answer 3.4:   The BBAIRS Settlement Rate is a set of Libor interest rates for several major currencies, which is published daily by *Telerate* on behalf of the British Bankers' Association on screen pages 3740–50, for use in refixing the floating interest rates on interest rate swaps (it is also used to settle FRAs). BBAIRS rates are available for monthly maturities between one and 12 months.

Answer 3.5:   A arranger   I   arrange swap between two end-users without participating

B market-maker   III commitment to quote two-way prices and deal at those prices

C assignment broker II selling swaps in which one is a counterparty to third parties

D broker   I   arrange swap between two end-users without participating

Answer 3.6: A bank paying fixed interest in a US dollar swap would typically warehouse (hedge) by buying *US Treasury securities*. If interest rates fall, the matching swap with which the bank eventually hedges the existing swap would pay the bank a lower fixed interest rate than it is currently paying, thereby locking in a loss. The hedge provided by the securities would however compensate for most of this loss, as the price of the securities would increase if interest rates fall. The purchase of the Treasury securities would be financed from the cash proceeds received in exchange for lending them temporarily (usually overnight) in a *repo (sale-and-repurchase agreement)*: a rate of interest, the repo rate, is paid on the cash received.

Answer 3.7: The bank in Question 3.6 above used US Treasury securities financed through a repo to hedge its swap. This type of warehouse leaves the bank exposed to two types of interest rate risk. First, the Treasury securities only hedge the benchmark yield component of the swap rate and not the *swap spread*. Second, the cost of the repo would be met from the floating interest received through the swap. As this is usually set at six-month Libor, while repos are usually overnight, there will be an element of *basis risk*.

Answer 3.8: The only practical way of hedging swap spread risk is with a *matching* (reverse) swap, which pays fixed interest incorporating a swap spread.

Answer 3 9: The payer of fixed interest through a coupon swap has *bought* a swap spread. If swap spreads narrow, the payer will *lose*, because a subsequent reverse swap would pay it a lower fixed interest rate than it is currently paying through the existing swap (assuming the benchmark yield does not rise and offset the narrowing spreads).

Answer 3.10: There are three basic techniques which are available to close out a swap position:

1 *reversal*: putting on a matching swap to hedge the existing swap.

2 *termination*: cancellation of a swap contract. This will involve a cash payment from one counterparty to another to compensate for the loss of expected profits on the swap.

3 *assignment*: the sale by a counterparty of its participation in a swap contract to a third party. The swap ceases to exist for the seller. The sale depends on the other existing counterparty agreeing to the new counterparty. As with a termination, an assignment involves a cash payment to compensate for the loss of expected profits on the swap: this time, between the seller and the buyer of the swap.

4 Pricing and valuing swaps

Pricing and valuation

Price

The **pricing** of interest rate swaps is the setting of the fixed interest rate for new coupon swaps or the margins between floating interest rates for new basis swaps. As pricing is concerned with new swaps, it is usually performed by drawing on current market swap rates. The factors which determine current market swap rates were described in the previous chapter on *Trading Swaps*.

Value

The **valuation** of interest rate swaps is the assessment of the net worth of the two future interest streams to be exchanged through the swap.

Par swaps

To appreciate the potential difference between price and value, it is necessary to understand that the value of a generic swap priced at current market rates (said to be priced at **par**) should be *zero*. In other words, for such a swap, there should be no difference between the value of the fixed interest stream and the value of the floating interest counterstream which will be exchanged through the swap. The value of both streams is expressed in terms of their *net present value* (NPV), which is the sum of the payments, where each is discounted to account for differences in the time value of money. Of course, the value of the fixed interest stream is known (because payments are fixed at the start of the swap), whereas the value of the floating interest stream is based on *expected* future interest rates (because payments are only fixed at the start of each successive interest period). Neither counterparty should rationally agree to a swap in which they expect to make a loss, ie, in which the net present value of their payments exceeds the net present value of their receipts. Of course, the net present values depend on expectations of future floating interest rates.

A neutral assumption about future interest rates is to use forward-forward interest rates). These are based on current cash interest rates. Therefore, generic swaps priced at current cash interest rates at par should have zero value.

Off-market swaps

Off- market swaps have non-zero values because:

■ they are not priced at par — ie, at current market rates — but at so-called **off-market** prices;

■ in the case of a coupon swap, although it might be priced at par when transacted, it is likely to diverge from current market swap rates as the fixed interest rate which constitutes the price becomes dated (a basis swap, on the other hand, returns to par and zero value each time the floating interest rates are reset at new current market levels).

Cash adjustment with off-market swaps

Off-market swaps are commonly used for **cash adjustment** purposes. Such swaps can be used to exchange payments at rates which are intended to match particular cash flow profiles on underlying transactions, rather than current market levels. An upfront cash payment is made between the counterparties to compensate for the difference between the off-market price of the swap and its value at current market rates. This payment may itself be part of the cash flow profile.

Valuing swaps for termination and

Apart from being used to calculate compensating upfront payments on off-market swaps, valuation is used when coupon swaps are terminated or assigned (see the previous section on *Trading Swaps*). As noted already, coupon swaps priced at par when transacted tend to become off-market as their fixed interest rates become outdated. Terminating or assigning a swap will deprive one of the counterparties of an expected gain between the fixed interest stream and the floating interest counterstream. Compensation equal to the value of the swap should be paid in cash.

Valuing generic term swaps

The rest of this chapter focuses on the valuation of generic par swaps. Valuing non-generic swaps is covered in the Workbook in this series on *Financial Engineering with Swaps*.

As noted already, the value of a swap is the difference between the NPVs of the two future interest cash flows being swapped.

■ For *payers* of fixed interest through a swap, the value of the swap is:

NPV (floating interest) – NPV (fixed interest)

■ For *receivers* of fixed interest through a swap, the value of the swap is:

NPV (fixed interest) – NPV (floating interest)

Valuing future fixed interest cash flows

Calculating the NPV of future fixed interest cash flows is straightforward as these future payments are known in advance. Because a stream of fixed interest payments is a series of constant amounts, it can be treated as an *annuity*. The NPV of an annuity is given by:

$$\text{PMT.} \left[\frac{1 - (1 + \frac{R}{f.100})^{-n}}{\frac{R}{f.100}} \right] \qquad (1)$$

Where   PMT = amount of fixed interest payment

R = discount rate

f = frequency of payments per year

n = number of payments during the swap

An example

Take a two-year swap priced at 9.125%pa, with a notional principal amount of £5m and semi-annual fixed interest payments. Assume the current two-year bond yield is 8.75%pa.

The amount of each fixed interest payment is:

£5,000,000 x (9.125/200) = £228,125

The NPV is therefore:

$$228{,}125 . \left[\dfrac{1 - \left(1 + \dfrac{8.75}{200}\right)^{-4}}{\dfrac{8.75}{200}} \right]$$

= £820,802

Valuing future floating interest cash flows

As explained already, in calculating the NPV of the interest cash flows through a swap, the size of each future *fixed* cash flow through a coupon swap is known from the start of the swap, but the size of each future *floating* cash flow is not known until the start of the particular interest period to which it applies (when the floating index is reset for that period). The solution adopted by the swap market is to use *forward-forward* interest rates to calculate future floating interest. These rates can be calculated from cash interest rates at the start of the swap. Because they are implied from cash rates, forward-forward interest rates represent a *neutral* solution to the problem of valuing future floating interest. They are not explicit forecasts of future rates and the interest rate that actually comes to prevail when the relevant period comes around may be different.

In practice, forward-forward interest rates are factored into the valuation of swaps, not directly as interest cash flows, but *indirectly* in terms of the notional principal amounts (NPAs) which generate those interest cash flows. For each cash flow, it is assumed that the NPA of the swap is borrowed at the start of the relevant interest period by the counterparty paying floating interest through the swap and lent by the counterparty receiving floating interest. It is also assumed that exactly the same NPA is repaid at the end of the interest period. The payer of floating interest through the swap is thus represented as paying interest on the notional borrowing, until it is cancelled by the notional repayment; and vice versa for the receiver of floating interest through the swap. This approach recalls the fact that an interest rate swap replicates the interest cash flows which are produced by a combination of a cash asset and a cash liability (see *Part One* on *The Swap Mechanism*). The approach is illustrated in Diagram 41 below.

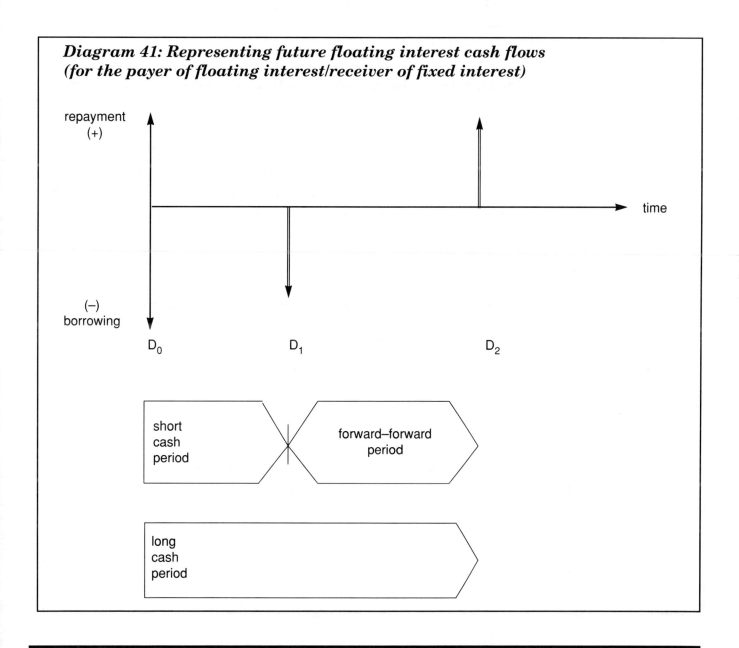

Diagram 41: Representing future floating interest cash flows (for the payer of floating interest/receiver of fixed interest)

When the notional borrowing (at D_1 in the diagram above) and its repayment (at D_2) are each discounted back to present values (at D_0), being of different signs, they largely cancel out. This result means that the method is consistent with there being no exchange of principal in an interest rate swap. The residual difference between the present values of the notional borrowing and repayment is in fact equal to the present value of the interest paid on the notional borrowing for the future interest period (D_{1-2}). Thus, in calculating the NPV of future interest cash flows through a swap, the use of NPAs at the start and end of each future interest period has the same net cash flow impact as direct inclusion of interest cash flows. The arithmetic behind this equation may be summarised as:

PV (borrowing at D_1) + PV (repayment at D_2) = NPV (interest for D_{1-2})   (3)

In the case of a swap with several interest periods, the NPAs at the start and end of each interest period largely offset each other. For example, take a two-year coupon swap involving a six-month floating interest rate. The floating interest payments would be represented as illustrated in Diagram 42 below.

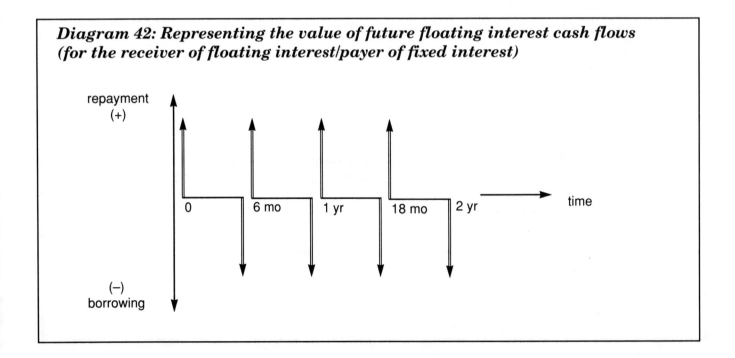

Diagram 42: Representing the value of future floating interest cash flows (for the receiver of floating interest/payer of fixed interest)

It can be seen that all NPAs cancel out except for the very first and very last, as illustrated in Diagram 43.

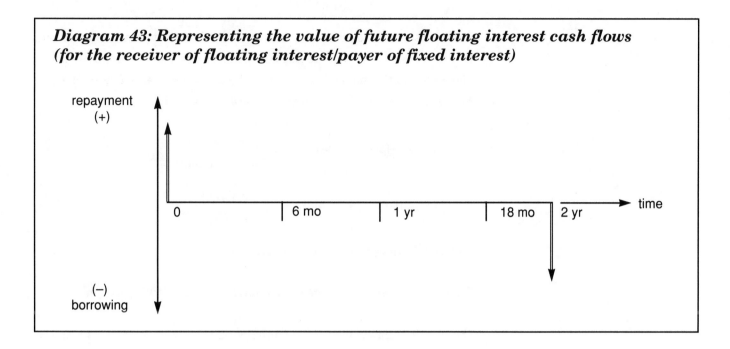

Diagram 43: Representing the value of future floating interest cash flows (for the receiver of floating interest/payer of fixed interest)

The value of the floating interest cash flows for an entire swap is therefore very conveniently represented by the sum of the NPA at the start of the swap and the same amount (but with a different sign) at the end of the swap. For generic swaps, which start immediately or out of spot, the present value of the NPA at the start of the swap is:

$$PV(NPA_1) = \frac{NPA_1}{\dfrac{discount\ rate}{100} \times \dfrac{0}{365}} = NPA_1 \qquad (4)$$

Consequently, for a generic swap, the value of floating interest cash flows is given simply by:

$$NPV\ (floating\ interest) = NPA_1 + PV(NPA)_2 \qquad (5)$$

An example

Take a one-year £100m coupon swap involving six-month Libor.

■ Calculating forward-forward interest rates.

Libor for this future period is taken to be the forward-forward interest rate for the period. To calculate the forward-forward rate, it is necessary to know six-month and 12-month Libor. Assume these rates are 10%pa and 11%pa, respectively. The forward-forward rate is:

$$(1+\text{forward--forward rate}) = \frac{(1+12\text{mo cash rate})}{(1+6\text{mo cash rate})} \qquad (6)$$

$$(1+\text{forward--forward rate}) = \frac{(1+11/100)}{(1+10/200)} \qquad (7)$$

$$\text{forward--forward rate} = 11.42\%\text{pa} \qquad (8)$$

The floating interest at six months would be £100m x (10/200) = £5m.

The floating interest at 12 months would be £100m x (11.42/100) = £5,714.286.

The present values (at 10% and 11% respectively) are £4,761,905 and £5,148,005. The NPV of the floating interest stream is therefore £9,909,910.

■ Using notional principal amounts.

To replicate the value of future floating interest cash flows, NPAs of £100m are recorded at the start and end of the swap and then discounted. The first amount does not need to be discounted (because the day count is 0). Discounting the last amount (at 11%) produces a present value of £90,090,090. The NPV is therefore £9,909,910 (= £100,000,000 – £90,090,090), the same as the result obtained by using forward-forward interest rates. This calculation is illustrated in the table below.

Item	0 months	12 months
notional principal amounts	+100,000,000	–100,000,000
cash rates	n/a	11%
present values	+100,000,000	–90,090,090
net present value	+9,909,910	

Valuing the whole swap

Having seen how the value of the future floating interest cash flows through a swap is calculated, it is possible to summarise the method for valuing both fixed and floating interest cash flows. Including the NPV of the fixed interest cash flows through the swap:

$$\text{NPV(swap)} = \text{NPA} - \text{PV(NPA)} - \sum_{t=1}^{n} \text{PV}(C_t) \tag{9}$$

where C_t = coupon or fixed interest cash flow at the end of interest period t

Given that the value of a generic par swap is zero, equation (6) above becomes:

$$\text{NPV(swap)} = \text{NPA} - \text{PV(NPA)} - \sum_{t=1}^{n} \text{PV}(C_t) = 0 \tag{10}$$

$$\text{PV(NPA)} + \sum_{t=1}^{n} \text{PV}(C_t) = \text{NPA} \tag{11}$$

From this equation, it is possible to calculate the fixed interest rate which should be quoted for the swap (if it is generic and par).

An example

Take the swap in the earlier example. Assume there is one fixed interest cash flow (C).

$$\text{PV(NPA)} + \text{PV(C)} = \text{NPA} \tag{12}$$

$$\pounds 90{,}090{,}090 + \text{PV(C)} = \pounds 100{,}000{,}000 \tag{13}$$

$$\therefore \text{PV(C)} = \pounds 9{,}909{,}910 \tag{14}$$

As the NPV of the fixed interest cash flow is £9,909,910, the nominal fixed interest cash flow at the end of the swap should be £11,000,000 (if £9,909,910 is compounded for one year at 11.00%pa), which gives a swap price of 11.00%pa. This is of course the same as the value of 12-month Libor, as it must be if the swap has zero value. This is the price at which the swap can be transacted, without the need for an extra payment between the swap counterparties.

Discounting to net present value

The next issue in valuation is what interest rates to use to discount the cash flows in swaps back to NPV. Yields-to-maturity (YTM) are average discount rates applying to series of future cash flows on fixed-income bonds. YTM is therefore not an accurate rate to use in discounting unrelated individual future cash flows (unless the yield curve is flat). The appropriate rates to use for discounting are *spot* or *zero coupon* interest rates, which is why the method of valuation described in this chapter is sometimes called *zero coupon pricing*.

Discout factors

Discount rates are normally presented in the form of reciprocal fractions called **discount factors**. For n years the discount factor is:

$$\frac{1}{1 + \left(\frac{\text{discount rate}}{100} \times \frac{\text{day count}}{\text{annual basis}} \right)^n} \tag{15}$$

A discount factor represents the present value of one unit of money due at a future date. Discount factors are a convenience: they allow discounting to be performed by multiplication by a single factor. Thus, to calculate the present value of any future cash flow, it is simply multiplied by the discount factor for the relevant maturity. In the example above, the discount factor applying to the one-year period of the swap is $1/(1 + 11\%) = 0.9009009$: multiplying this by the notional principal amount of £100m produces a present value of £90,090,090. A series of discount factors is called a **discount function** and is used like a yield curve. Using discount factors, equation (6) above can be recast as:

$$NPV(swap) = [NPA - (NPA.F_n)] - \sum_{t=1}^{n} (C_t . F_t) \tag{16}$$

where F_t = discount factor at time t
F_n = discount factor at maturity

Valuing generic money market swaps

Swaps, futures and FRAs

It was explained in *Using Swaps* in *Part Two* that it is possible to arbitrage between swaps and other derivative instruments like futures and FRAs, because they all perform the same function. For the same reason, it is also possible to hedge swaps with futures and FRAs. The use of futures and FRAs to arbitrage and hedge swaps means that the price of the latter depends closely on the interest rates offered by the other instruments. However, the limited range of liquid futures and FRAs in terms of tenors typically restricts arbitrage and hedging up to two years, with *money market swaps*.

Strips

It was also explained in *Part Two* that futures and FRAs cover single interest periods only, while swaps are multi-period instruments. Therefore, in order to arbitrage and hedge between money market swaps on the one hand, and futures and FRAs on the other, it is necessary to transact a *strip* or series of consecutive futures or FRAs. To calculate the price of the strip as a whole, the individual interest rates on the futures or FRAs are *stripped*, meaning the individual rates are compounded to produce a single average rate for the period.

Stripping futures and FRAs

A good approximation for stripping futures and FRAs is a simple serial compounding:

$$([n \sqrt{ (1 + \frac{F_1}{100} \frac{D}{B}) \ (1 + \frac{F_2}{100} \frac{D}{B}) \ldots (1 + \frac{F_z}{100} \frac{D}{B})}] - 1) \ (\frac{D}{B} . 100) \qquad (17)$$

where

F_1 = current cash interest rate
F_z = futures/FRA price for last period
D = day count
B = annual basis
n = number of years in the strip

Note that the first interest rate in the equation is the cash rate for the current period, which runs from the transaction date to the start of the first futures or FRA contract (futures and FRAs only cover forward-forward periods).

Mismatches with futures contract periods

A problem with stripping futures is that there are usually only four standard contract periods a year, which invariably means that futures do not exactly match but overlap the periods required by users. For example, the periods for the three-month sterling futures contract traded on Liffe start on 16 September 1992, 16 December 1992, 17 March 1993, 16 June 1993 and so on. Assume a user wishes to strip that futures contract for the period 16 October 1992 to 16 April 1993. What futures contracts should he use?

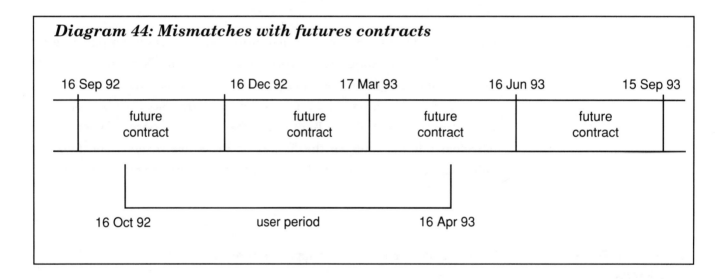

Diagram 44: Mismatches with futures contracts

The simplest technique to resolve the problem of mismatches with futures contract periods is to weight the number of each futures contract transacted by the proportion of the contract period covered by the required strip. In the example illustrated above, the weights would be 2:3:1 between the September 1992, December 1992 and March 1993 contracts.

An example   The information screen reproduced in Diagram 45 below is produced by *Thomson Financial Services* as part of the *MoneyData* service, which is disseminated on the *Telerate* network. It sets out indicative prices for US dollar interest rate swaps, as well as US dollar cash and other derivative instruments like futures and FRAs. The swap prices in the second and third columns should be in line with the futures prices in the last two columns.

Diagram 45: Information screen (Telerate page 8066)

MONEYDATA TFS (C) 92		US INT RATE SWAPS & FRAS		10/29		10:34	8066

[TSY-BEY]	[SWAP A/360-HI/LO]	STUB TO 12/16/92	3.28			[IMM EURO$]			
1YR	3.44	3.89	3.90/88	[SEMI 30/360]		[SPRD-HI/LO]			Z93	94.90
2YR	4.29	4.65		4.67		38		39/37	Z92	96.40	H94	94.67
3YR	4.75	5.29		5.29		54		57/53	H93	96.40	M94	94.30
4YR	5.27	5.78		5.77		50		53/48	M93	95.95	U94	94.01
5YR	5.79	6.15		6.14		35		38/33	U93	95.52	Z94	93.60

		[FRA BREAKEVENS (IMPLIED BY IMM STRIP)]					H95	93.49

[CASH LIBOR]			3MO		6MO		12MO		M95	93.27
O/N	3.00	1X4	3.61	1X7	3.62	1X13	ERR		U95	93.11
1MO	3.25	2X5	3.59	2X8	3.65	2X14	ERR		Z95	92.83
2MO	3.31	3X6	3.60	3X9	3.74	3X15	4.20		H96	92.80
3MO	3.63	4X7	3.60	4X10	3.81	4X16	4.34		M96	92.62
4MO	3.63	5X8	3.68	5X11	3.92	5X17	4.47		U96	92.49
6MO	3.63	6X9	3.83	6X12	4.08	6X18	4.61		Z96	92.29
9MO	3.75	9X12	4.28	9X15	4.57	9X21	5.03		H97	92.33
12MO	3.94	12X15	4.81	12X18	5.04	12X24	5.45		M97	92.19
									U97	92.09

NOTE: (I) - FOUR YEAR TSY IS INTERPOLATED YLD.

Libor for 1 month (31 days) and 2 months (61 days)

1-year swap price

futures prices which are used to calculate the 1-year strip, where Z92 is the December 1992 contract for settlement on 16 December, H93 is the March 1993 contract for settlement on 17 March, etc.

For example, the one-year swap price of 3.89 (shown at the top of the second column) should be in line with the price of the contiguous futures contracts. The implied price for this swap can be calculated by plugging in Libor for the period until the first futures contract (16 December)[1] and then the interest rates implied from the prices of the strip of futures from December 1992 (contract Z92) to September 1993 (contract U93) into equation (17):

$$\left(\left[\sqrt{\left(1+\frac{3.28}{100}\cdot\frac{48}{360}\right)\left(1+\frac{3.60}{100}\cdot\frac{91}{360}\right)\left(1+\frac{3.60}{100}\cdot\frac{91}{360}\right)\left(1+\frac{4.05}{100}\cdot\frac{91}{360}\right)\left(1+\frac{4.48}{100}\cdot\frac{44}{360}\right)}\right]-1\right)\left(\frac{365}{360}\cdot100\right)$$

(18)

$$=\left(\left(\left(1.00437\times1.0091\times1.0091\times1.01024\times1.0055\right)-1\right)\frac{36500}{360}\right.$$

(19)

$$=3.94\%\text{ per annum}$$

(20)

Notes
1. Libor for the period to the first futures contract (which covers 48 days) is interpolated from the one (31 days) and two-month (61 days) Libor rates:

$$3.31-\left(\frac{3.31-3.25}{30\text{ days}}\times17\text{ days}\right)=3.28\%\text{pa}$$

Self-Study Exercises: <u>Questions</u>   Part 4

Question 4.1:   How are future floating interest rates calculated when a swap is valued?

Question 4.2:   What is a *par* swap? What is a *non-par* swap called?

Question 4.3:   From the following cash interest rates on three-month sterling deposits and prices for sterling futures contracts (on three-month sterling interest rates), calculate the price of a one-year sterling money market coupon swap to mature on 22 June 1993, in which the floating interest rate is three-month sterling Libor. Assume today is 22 June 1992.

three-month cash sterling Libor   *10.0625%*
   (matures 22 September 1992 after 92 days)

nearby short sterling futures contract   *90.25*
   (settles 16 September 1992 after 91 days)

next short sterling futures contract   *90.50*
   (settles 16 December 1992 after 91 days)

next short sterling futures contract   *90.72*
   (settles 17 March 1993 after 91 days)

next short sterling futures contract   *90.91*
   (settles 16 June 1993 after 91 days)

NB: *The three-month cash and the nearby futures contract overlap by six days (17–22 September 1992). The swap and the furthest futures contract also overlap by six days (17–22 June 1993).*

Question 4.4:   What is the net present value of the floating interest due through a coupon swap with a notional principal value of £55m and a period of 4.5 years remaining to maturity? Assume the current swap rate for 4.5-year sterling coupon swaps is 10.125% per annum.

Question 4.5:   If the fixed interest due through the swap in Question 4.4 is priced at 10.625% per annum, paid semi-annually, what is the value of the swap?

Self-Study Exercises: <u>Answer</u>   Part 4

Answer 4.1:   It is usual to assume that future, and therefore unknown, floating-interest rates are given by the *forward-forward* interest rates for the future periods implied from cash interest rates.

Answer 4.2:   A *par* swap is a *generic swap priced at current market rates which therefore has a value of zero. A generic swap is a coupon swap with (1) a spot start, (2) regular interest payments, (3) fixed notional principal amount and (4) no special risk features (such as options). Zero value means that the net present value of the fixed interest to be paid through the swap and the floating interest expected to be received through the swap are equal.*

A *non-par* swap is called an *off-market* swap, as it is priced at rates other than those currently prevailing on the market.

Answer 4.3:   During the period of the one-year swap, the instruments generating the interest rates to be used in pricing the swap mature in following sequence:

today	*22 June 1992*
nearby future settles	*16 September 1992*
three-month cash sterling matures	*22 September 1992*
next short sterling future settles	*16 December 1992*
next short sterling future settles	*17 March 1993*
next short sterling future settles	*16 June 1993*
one-year swap matures	*22 June 1993*

(Answer 4.3 ctd)

The interest rates and day counts for different periods are summarised in the diagram below. The rates attached to the futures contracts have been implied from their prices.

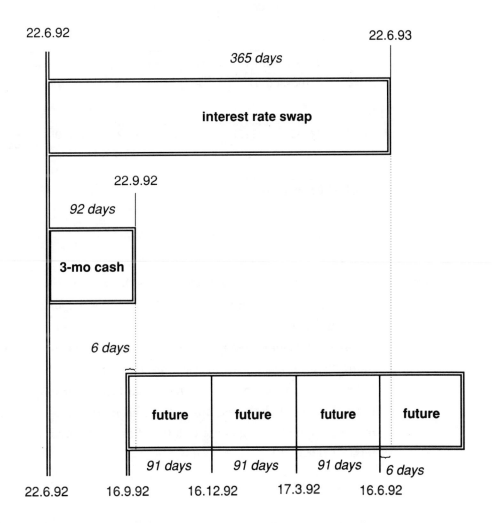

Interest rate swaps

(Answer 4.3 ctd) The interest rates and day counts can be plugged into equation (17) for a futures or FRA strip given in *Part Four*:

$$\left[n\sqrt{\left(1+\frac{F_1.D}{100.B}\right)\ \left(1+\frac{F_2.D}{100.B}\right)\ \left(1+\frac{F_3.D}{100.B}\right)\ \left(1+\frac{F_4.D}{100.B}\right)\ \left(1+\frac{F_5.D}{100.B}\right)} - 1\right]\frac{D}{B}.100$$

where n = number of floating interest periods
  F = interest rate on cash or future
  D = day count of instrument
  B = annual basis (365 for sterling)

$$\left(\left[4\sqrt{\left|1+\frac{10.0625*92}{100*365}\right|\left|1+\frac{9.75*85}{100*365}\right|\left|1+\frac{9.50*91}{100*365}\right|\left|1+\frac{9.28*91}{100*365}\right|\left|1+\frac{9.09*6}{100*365}\right|}\right]-1\right)\frac{365}{365}.100$$

$$= \left(\left[4\sqrt{1.02536 * 1.02271 * 1.02368 * 1.02314 * 1.00149}\right]-1\right)\frac{365}{365}.100$$

$$= \left(\left[4\sqrt{1.09996}\right]-1\right)\frac{365}{365}.100$$

$$= 9.64\%\,pa$$

Answer 4.4: It was explained in *Part Four* that future floating interest rates in a swap are assumed, for the purposes of valuing swaps, to be given by the *forward-forward* interest rates for the future periods which are implied from cash interest rates. However, it was also explained that forward-forward interest rates are factored into the valuation of swaps indirectly in terms of their notional principal amounts (NPAs). The present value of the NPA at the start of the swap (which is in fact equal to the nominal NPA), minus the present value of the same amount at the maturity of the swap, is equal to the net present value of the amounts of future floating interest calculated at forward-forward interest rates.

NPV(swap) = NPA + PV(NPA)

The present value of the NPA of £55m discounted at the current swap rate of 10.125% per annum over 4.5 years is £35,634,941. Therefore:

NPV(swap) = £55,000,000 – £35,634,941 = £19,365,059

130

Answer 4.5: The value of a swap is the difference between the net present value of the fixed interest paid through the swap and the net present value of the floating interest expected to be paid through the swap.

NPV (fixed interest) – NPV (floating interest)

The net present value of the fixed interest is in effect an annuity and is given by:

$$\text{PMT}. \left[\frac{1 - (1 + \frac{R}{f.100})^{-n}}{\frac{R}{f.100}} \right]$$

where PMT = amount of fixed interest payment
(10.625% x 0.5 x £55m = £2,921,875)
R = discount rate
(the current swap rate, ie 10.125% per annum)
f = frequency of payment
(semi-annual, ie f = 2)
n = number of fixed interest payments
(= f x number of years to maturity, ie 9)

$$\text{£2,921,875} \left[\frac{1 - (1 + \frac{10.125}{200})^{-9}}{\frac{10.125}{200}} \right] = \text{£19,735,875}$$

The net present value of the floating interest was calculated in Answer 4.4 and was £35,634,941.

The value of the swap (to the counterparty receiving fixed interest) is therefore:

£19,735,875 – £19,365,059 = –£370,816

5 Swap risk and regulation

Swap risk

Types of swap risk

Previous chapters of this Workbook have examined the exposure which interest rate swaps open up to *interest rate risk*. Interest rate risk includes *swap spread risk*, *basis risk* and other *mismatch risks* found in trying to hedge the exposure on swaps. Even if the risks taken through a swap turn out to be profitable, there is still the additional *credit risk* that the interest profit might not be paid over by the counterparty. This chapter examines the credit risk in swaps.

The impact of credit risk on swaps

The impact of credit risk on counterparties to (off-balance sheet) derivative instruments like swaps should be distinguished from the impact in the case of (on-balance sheet) cash instruments. In the case of derivatives, the credit risk is on *interest only*; on cash instruments, credit risk threatens *principal* and *interest*.

The interest payments at risk in a swap can take a number of forms, depending on the purpose for which the swap is being used:

- if the swap is being used to *hedge*, the default of one counterparty will leave the other exposed to the interest rate risk which was being hedged and an *actual* cost if that risk is realised;

- if the swap is being used to take *risk*, the default of one counterparty will deprive the other of the opportunity for making a profit on future interest rate movements, which is an *opportunity* rather than an *actual* cost;

- if the swap is being used to *arbitrage*, the default of one counterparty will deprive the other of the opportunity for making a profit on future interest rate movements, which is also an *opportunity* cost: however, the remaining side of the arbitrage may be in loss, producing an *actual* cost.

Measuring the impact of credit risk on swaps

Given that the credit risk on a swap is one of non-payment of interest, the *impact* on swap counterparties of credit risk being realised is often expressed in terms of the concept of **default risk**, where:

default risk = credit risk x interest rate risk   (1)

credit risk = probability of default

The measurement of the *credit risk* component in the above equation involves the application of the standard techniques of credit analysis developed for use across the financial sector.

To analyse the *interest rate risk* component of the default risk on swaps, it is necessary to distinguish between:

■   *current* **risk:** the interest loss which would be suffered in the event of an immediate default;

■   *future* **risk:** the interest loss which would be suffered in the event of a *future* default (between now and the maturity of the swap).

The impact of an immediate swap default can be estimated with certainty. The impact of a future default, on the other hand, is uncertain, because the date of default and future interest rates are unknown.

Measuring current interest rate risk

The interest loss which would be suffered at the time of an immediate default can be measured using the methods of swap valuation described in *Part Four*. However, in practice, valuation for the purposes of credit risk measurement tends to be much simpler than for pricing. In assessing the credit risk on coupon swaps, only the fixed interest cash flows are usually valued. The usual method of valuing swaps for credit risk assessment assumes that swap counterparties will immediately seek to *replace* swaps on which there has been a default with new swaps of the same maturity, or *terminate* or *assign* any matching swaps which are left exposed by the default. Because floating interest rates are reset periodically and frequently, it is assumed that a replacement swap will not represent much of a disturbance to the floating interest cash flow (in reality, the mismatching of reset dates that might result when a swap is replaced can have serious consequences).

If a replacement swap can be found which is an exact replica of the original swap, not least in terms of its price, then the default will have had no impact and credit risk can be seen to have been zero. In practice, swap rates will almost certainly have moved since the original swap was transacted and the current interest rate risk is therefore equivalent to the **replacement cost** of the defaulted swap, which is given by the differential between the original and replacement swap prices, over the remaining time to maturity of the swap. Thus, for the purposes of estimating default risk, the interest rate risk on a swap is:

interest rate risk = NPV (original fixed interest) – NPV (defaulted fixed interest) (2)

In practice, a replacement swap is usually assumed to be transacted at the price of the *original* swap. As the original price will have become an off-market rate, compensation for the difference between the original swap rate and current swap rate must be paid in the form of an upfront cash payment:

■   if swap rates have *risen* between the transaction of a swap and default, the cash payment needed to compensate for the fact that a replacement swap at the original price pays a below-market rate is due to the *receiver* of fixed interest;

■   if swap rates have *fallen*, the cash payment needed to offset the fact that a replacement swap at the original price pays an above-market rate is due to the *payer* of fixed interest.

As shown in equation (2) above, the cash payment representing the replacement cost of a swap is the difference between the net present value (NPV) of the stream of fixed interest cash flows calculated at the original swap rate and the NPV of the stream calculated at the replacement swap rate for the remaining time to maturity. As the stream of fixed interest cash flows through a swap is not accompanied by payments of principal, it is in effect an *annuity* and its NPV is:

$$\text{NPV(fixed interest)} = \text{PMT.} \left[\frac{1 - (1 + \frac{R}{f.100})^{-n}}{\frac{R}{f.100}} \right] \qquad (3)$$

where PMT = amount of fixed interest payment
R = discount rate
f = frequency of payment per annum
n = number of fixed payments remaining before maturity

An example

Take a $50m coupon swap with 10 years remaining to maturity. Assume the fixed rate is 12%, paid annually. Thus:

PMT = $6m (=$50m x 12%)
R = 12%
f = 1
n = 10 (= 1 payment a year x 10 years)

The NPV of the stream of fixed interest cash flows at current market interest rates is:

$$\$6,000,000 \left[\frac{1 - (1 + \frac{12}{100})^{-10}}{\frac{12}{100}} \right] = \$33,901,338 \qquad (4)$$

Assume the current 10-year US dollar swap rate is 10%pa: this would be the price of a replacement for the existing swap. The NPV of such a swap would be:

$$\$6,000,000 \left[\frac{1 - (1 + \frac{10}{100})^{-10}}{\frac{10}{100}} \right] = \$36,867,403 \qquad (5)$$

The replacement cost of the swap would, for the purposes of measuring default risk, be given by the difference between the NPV calculated at the original swap rate in equation (4) and the NPV calculated at the replacement swap rate in equation (5), which is $2,966,064.

The process of comparing the original price of an existing swap and current swap rates in order to calculate replacement cost is called **marking to market**.

Measuring future interest rate risk

Calculating the replacement cost of a swap using *current* interest rate risk is based on the assumption of immediate default and ignores the possibility that a default will occur at some time in the *future*. Future swap replacement costs cannot be known with certainty. Expected future replacement costs are said to be stochastic or probabilistic, meaning there is a range of possible costs, each with a different probability. In practice, this problem is taken into account by using the weighted average of a range of future replacement costs judged to be likely over the remaining period to maturity, where the weight for each possible replacement cost is its probability.

This statistical approach to the estimation of future swap replacement costs requires the specification of the distribution of the probabilities of future interest rates (ie, what probability is attached to each possible future interest rate). The parameters of probability distributions usually reflect estimates of interest rate volatility based on historical data. In practice, swap counterparties tend to adapt option pricing models.

Measuring the impact of credit risk on swap portfolios

As with any statistical procedure, the accuracy of probability-weighted average future replacement costs improves if they are applied, not just to individual swaps, but to a *portfolio* of many swaps. The statistical measure of the overall interest rate risk on a swap portfolio tends to be lower than the sum of individually-calculated risks. This reduction reflects the effect of diversification across a portfolio (see the next section on *Managing Credit Risk on Swaps*).

Change in the impact of credit risk over time

At the time an interest rate swap is transacted, its value is zero, implying that there is no current replacement cost, which means there is also no current interest rate risk and no current default risk. As noted already, future replacement cost depends on the direction in which interest rates move in the future. This is stochastic and cannot be known with certainty. However, there are three tendencies which change the interest rate risk on a swap in more deterministic ways as it moves to maturity:

■   as the life of a swap moves to maturity, the number of interest payments which are due through the swap declines: this automatically reduces the interest rate risk on the swap;

■   as the life of a swap moves to maturity, current swap rates become increasingly less likely to diverge from or converge with the price at which the swap has been transacted: this will tend to reduce further changes in the replacement cost of the swap;

■   where there are *payment mismatches* in a swap (eg, fixed interest may be paid annually and floating interest semi-annually, default may leave one counterparty having made a gross payment without receiving the entire amount of the offsetting counterpayment: the credit risk on the interest cash flows through a swap will therefore increase each time a mismatched payment is outstanding to a counterparty.

Risk capital requirements for swaps

Basle Agreement

In July 1988, the Committee on Banking Regulation and Supervisory Practices of the Group of Ten industrialised countries (the G-10) — which meets regularly at the Bank for International Settlements (BIS) at Basle in Switzerland to co-ordinate the supervision of international banks — published its *Proposals for International Convergence of Capital Measurement and Capital Standards*. The objective is to ensure that, from the end of 1992 (mid-1989 in the UK), standards of capital adequacy for international commercial banks have *converged*. Every international commercial bank should have risk capital:

■ of commonly-defined quality;

■ covering at least 8% of credit risk (the so-called *Basle ratio*);

■ including credit risk on and off the balance sheet, as measured according to common rules.

The *Basle Convergence Agreement* (more usually called the *Basle Agreement* or *Basle Accord*) currently only covers *credit risk*: work is continuing to include what the authorities term *investment risk*, which includes interest rate and exchange rate risks.

Calculating risk capital requirements on swaps

The method prescribed by the Basle Agreement for determining the minimum risk capital requirement for off-balance sheet instruments reflects the analysis of risk set out in the previous section, by implicitly distinguishing:

■ default risk as a function of (1) *credit* risk (probability of default) and (2) *interest rate* risk (the loss due to default);

■ interest rate risk as a function of (1) *current* risk and (2) *future* risk.

Calculating credit risk for Basle

Credit risk is classified under the Basle Agreement into five bands, largely defined by (1) reference to whether a counterparty is official or private and (2) whether it is based in a country within the OECD. Each band has a **risk weight** measuring the probability of default for the purposes of calculating risk capital requirements. For the purposes of calculating the credit risk on interest rate and exchange rate instruments, including swaps, the 100% risk weight has been reduced to 50%. This means that there are in fact only *four* bands for interest rate and exchange rate instruments.

Basle risk weights

0%	cash
	bullion
	loans to OECD governments/central banks
	loans to non-OECD governments/central banks in own currency
10%	loans on the UK discount market
	short-term fixed-income debt on OECD central governments
	floating-rate debt on OECD central governments
	funded short-term debt of non-OECD central governments
20%	long-term fixed-income debt on OECD governments
	funded long-term debt on non-OECD central governments
	claims on multilateral development banks
	claims on OECD-incorporated banks
	funded short-term claims on non-OECD-incorporated banks
	claims on OECD non-commercial public sector organisations
50%	residential mortgages
100%	claims on non-bank private sector
	long-term claims on non-OECD banks
	unfunded & foreign currency claims on non-OECD governments
	claims on OECD public sector commercial companies
	claims on non-OECD public sector
	fixed assets
	property
	aggregate net short open foreign exchange positions

NB: Short-term means below 1 year and long-term means 1 year and longer; both refer to residual maturities. Funded means funded in the same currency. The 100% risk weight is only 50% for interest rate and exchange rate instruments, including swaps.

Calculating interest rate risk for Basle

Interest rate risk under the Basle Agreement is calculated using one of two alternative methods. National supervisors are free to select the method to be applied in their country:

■ **current exposure method** calculates interest rate risk in terms of

— **current exposure**, which corresponds to current interest rate risk and is the *replacement cost* of a swap, measured by *marking to market*: where a default on a swap would benefit a counterparty and there is therefore no replacement cost, its current exposure is zero;

— **residual maturity** or **potential exposure**, which corresponds to future interest rate risk, is measured by one of the following **residual maturity weights** (sometimes called **add-ons**), expressed as a flat percentage of the notional principal amount of an instrument:

Residual maturity	Residual maturity weight
less than 1 year	0
more than 1 year	0.5% flat
basis swaps	0

■ **original exposure method** does not distinguish between current and future interest rate risk: interest rate risk is calculated in terms of fixed weights, expressed as percentages (flat and annual) of notional principal amounts, related to the *original* maturity of the swap:

Original maturity	Original maturity weight
less than 1 year	0.5% flat
1–2 years	1.0% flat
more than 2 years	1.0% per year beyond 2 years

Interest rate risk (calculated as either current or original exposure) is multiplied by credit risk (in the form of the Basle risk weights) to calculate the default risk on a swap or its **risk-adjusted balance**. The risk capital requirement for a swap is then 8% of this figure. The process of calculating the risk capital requirement for an interest rate swap under the Basle Agreement is illustrated in Diagram 46 below.

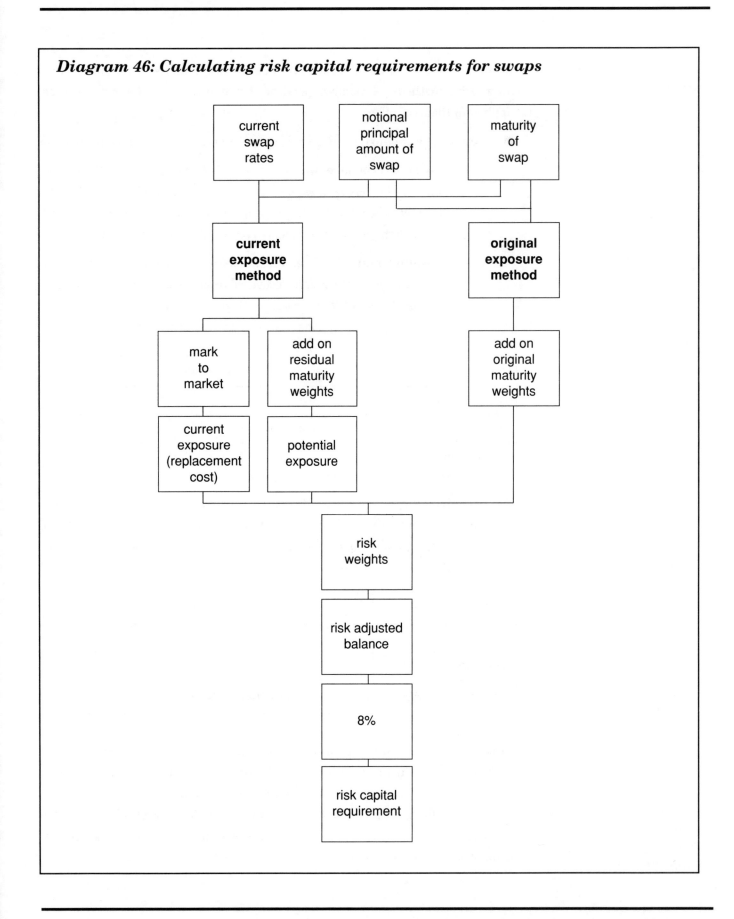

Diagram 46: Calculating risk capital requirements for swaps

An example   A simplified illustration of the calculation of the risk capital requirements for a swaps book under the current exposure method of the Basle Agreement is given in the table below.

Residual maturity	Less than 1 year	More than 1 year	Less than 1 year	More than 1 year	Less than 1 year	More than 1 year
notional principal amount	645.5	505.7	458.7	350.3	250.9	106.4
current exposure (NPA marked to market)	6.567	6.123	3.367	4.693	1.923	0.887
residual maturity weights	0%	0.5%	0%	0.5%	0%	0.5%
potential exposuure (weighted NPA)	0	2.529	0	1.752	0	0.532
total exposure	6.567	8.652	3.367	6.445	1.923	1.419
risk weights	0%	0%	20%	20%	50%	50%
risk adjusted balance	0	0	0.673	1.289	0.962	0.710
			1.962		1.672	
8% risk capital requirement	0	0	0.157		0.134	
			£0.291 (rounded)			

EC Directives

The European Commission has been seeking to harmonise prudential supervision within the European Community (EC) in support of the Single European Market programme and has promulgated or is about to promulgate a number of regulations on risk capital to be implemented in Member States. The relevant EC initiatives are:

■ the *Solvency Ratio Directive* (Council Directive 89/647/EEC) governing the minimum capital adequacy requirements on commercial banks to cover default risk: this largely follows the Basle Agreement;

■ the *Second Banking Co-ordination Directive* governing the initial minimum capital requirements on commercial banks;

■ the *Directive on Own Funds* (89/299/EEC) governing the definition of risk capital for commercial banks: this also largely follows the Basle Agreement;

■ the proposed *Directive on the Capital Adequacy of Investment Firms and Credit Institutions*, which would govern minimum capital requirements for investment banks; and *position risks* (eg, interest rate and exchange rate risks) for both commercial and investment banks; the definition of capital for investment banks largely follows the Own Funds Directive.

Managing credit risk on swaps

Netting

The dramatic growth in the size of the swap market has increasingly encouraged swap intermediaries to seek ways of containing their exposure to risk. The imposition by banking supervisors of risk capital requirements on derivative instruments such as interest rate swaps has generated particular interest in the containment of default risk as a way of ameliorating the burden of capital requirements. Proposals to limit default risk have centred on the procedure of **netting**.

Netting is the offsetting of several separate payments outstanding between the same two counterparties and the settlement of the overall difference as a single net amount paid in one direction rather than several gross amounts paid in both directions.

Netting generally occurs *within* individual swaps when interest payments between the counterparties occur on the same dates. Often payment frequencies will be rearranged to allow netting, eg annual fixed interest payments will be split and paid semi-annually to match semi-annual floating interest payments.

Netting *between* separate swaps (which is what the term 'netting' is usually taken to mean) is the netting of the *net present values* of separate swaps outstanding between the same two counterparties if one defaults. Netting between swaps can be achieved by:

- **novation** — with each new swap, a single new contract is created incorporating the new swap and all previous still-outstanding swaps: the ISDA master contracts achieve this by adding new swap agreements as appendices;

- **close-out** — a cross-default clause nets out all outstanding swaps between two counterparties in the event of one defaulting.

Market participants have sought to enforce netting in cases of default in order to limit their default risk. Without netting, the receivers or administrators of bankrupt companies can maintain swap contracts which are profitable from their point of view and default on unprofitable swaps, even if these contracts are with the same counterparty: the so-called practice of **cherry-picking.** The problem with netting is that there have been considerable doubts about the ability to enforce it in most jurisdictions. Netting can be construed as giving swap counterparties superior rights to other creditors and this is generally illegal. Little exists in the way of legislation or legal precedent to clarify the position. Although most swap contracts contain opinion from legal counsel in support of netting and much of the documentation work of ISDA has been directed at establishing the legal enforceability of netting, none of this is a substitute for an actual legal judgement. Ironically, the generally strong credit history of the swaps market has precluded such an opportunity.

In the US, the problem of netting appears to have been partially resolved by the enactment in August 1989 of the *Financial Institutions Reform, Recovery and Enforcement Act (FIRREA)* which recognised netting provisions in cases of insolvency involving US domestic banks and thrifts. This Act was clarified in June 1990 by an amendment to the *US Bankruptcy Code* which stated that netting would be enforceable against insolvent corporate end-users and non-bank swap dealers. However, the situation remains unresolved in the case of other countries and cross-border swap defaults.

Netting and capital adequacy

In view of the residual doubts about the legal enforceability of netting between domestic counterparties in most countries and the unresolved doubts about cross-border netting, the Basle-based Committee on Banking Regulation and Supervisory Practices has made only limited concessions to the argument that netting should be translated into lower risk capital requirements. The supervisory authorities distinguish between:

■ **netting** — meaning offsetting between swaps transacted between the same counterparties on the *same* day and in the same currency;

■ **set-off** — meaning offsetting between swaps transacted between the same counterparties on *different* days and in different currencies.

The Basle Agreement allows interest rate risk to be measured for the purposes of calculating default risk with netting by novation (netting between swaps transacted on the same day and in the same currency), but does not allow any set-off (netting between swaps transacted on different days and in different currencies). The general issue of netting was the subject of a consultative paper issued by the Basle Committee on Banking Supervision in May 1993, Its significance lies in the fact that the BIS, for the first time, recognises the effectiveness of bilateral close-out netting agreements in determining banks' capital standards.

Credit enhancement

Credit enhancement is any technique which reduces the default risk on transactions by providing protection against any loss due to default by a counterparty, but without actually reducing the credit risk (probability of default) on that counterparty. The principal techniques of credit enhancement are:

■   *collateralisation*;

■   *insurance* by a third party.

■   *guarantees* by highly creditworthy third parties.

Collateralisation

One or both swap counterparties are protected against loss due to a default by the other by the *pledging* of suitable assets (usually government securities or marketable collateralised assets).

There are two basic approaches to collateralisation:

■   the *weaker* counterparty posts collateral at the inception of a swap and subsequently adds further collateral to cover any increase above this initial amount in the value of the swap to the stronger counterparty;

■   *mutual* collateralisation: usually involving the posting of collateral at the inception of a swap by both counterparties and the subsequent addition of further collateral by either counterparty to cover any significant increase above the initial amount in the value of the swap or to cover a significant deterioration in their creditworthiness.

Collateralisation emerged in the US as a means of allowing thrifts and smaller regional banks to participate in the swap market. It remains most common in the US. Thrifts, which lend fixed-rate mortgages but usually fund at floating rates, are important natural users of interest rate swaps and have ready access to marketable collateralised assets, like mortgage-backed securities, to use as collateral.

Insurance

In March 1986, the World Bank group arranged an insurance facility with the Aetna Insurance Company of the US to cover up to 30–50% of the credit exposure on specified interest rate and cross-currency swaps with AA and A-rated counterparties. The limited cover is designed to allow the World Bank to replace swaps at current swap rates in the event of default. The World Bank pays a commitment fee and a variable exposure-related insurance premium. The insured credit exposure is marked to market weekly. The World Bank has subsequently arranged an insurance facility with Deutsche Bank.

The Aetna insurance facility effectively allowed the World Bank to circumvent a restriction imposed by its Executive Board limiting it to AAA-rated counterparties. This permitted the World Bank to diversify its swap portfolio, which had become concentrated on a very limited number of counterparties because of the credit risk restrictions. Insurance was anyway cheaper than intermediation by AAA-rated banks (of which there are a decreasing number).

Clearing house

Proposals for a clearing house to provide a centrally-organised exchange for the interbank trading of swaps have been under discussion for several years within ISDA. These proposals involve the translation of interest rate swaps into a highly-standardised instrument like futures and listed options. The clearing house would impose the sort of margining and daily mark-to-market requirements on counterparties which is found in futures exchanges. It would also step into deals once they had been struck, creating two new swaps in which it would act as counterparty to the original counterparties. As the clearing house would have its own capital endowment and be backed by the credit of its members, its intermediation would ensure the performance of contracts and significantly reduce their credit risk. The intermediation of the clearing house in all swap contracts and the standardisation of swap contracts traded through the clearing house would also allow netting to be enforced.

Firm proposals for a clearing house in French franc swaps with maturities of up to 12 years have been put forward by the private futures and options exchange, Optionsmarknad France, but have yet to materialise.

Objections to the proposals have centred on the comparative trading advantage which some strong swap counterparties believe they might surrender to weaker credits admitted to the clearing house and the support which stronger counterparties believe they would have to provide to the clearing house in the event of default by weaker members. There is also the question of the expense of establishing the clearing house. Additionally, in the US, there are a range of regulatory obstacles.

Regulation of the conduct of business in swaps in the UK

Bank of England Wholesale Markets Supervision

From 29 April 1988, *investment business* in the UK has been subject to the *Financial Services Act 1986* (FSA). This legislation was intended to establish a comprehensive framework of investor protection in the UK. Investment business includes all forms of non-credit financial intermediation: dealing in, arranging, advising on and managing investments. All financial intermediaries must be authorised and supervised by the *Securities and Investment Board (SIB)* or an authorised *Self-Regulatory Organisation (SRO)* or *Recognised Investment Exchange (RIE)*. Credit activities (traditional commercial banking) continue to be supervised by the Bank of England under the *Banking Act 1987*. The FSA is enforced by sanctions under criminal law, a civil law framework under which intermediaries can be sued by investors, if they breach the Act, and the threat of exclusion from investment business. The FSA, although designed to protect small investors, encompasses some professional markets such as that in Eurobonds. However, it was eventually decided that certain *wholesale* markets — in 'treasury' products, such as foreign exchange, bullion, money and related instruments (including interest rate swaps) — do not need the degree of investor protection offered by the FSA and should be exempted from the FSA, as they are composed of professional intermediaries fully aware of the risks to which they are exposed and have been traditionally supervised by the Bank of England. A special clause, Section 43, was drafted into the Act. Despite this exemption, however, the FSA forced the Bank of England to impose a more formal framework of supervision on the wholesale markets in the UK in order to stop Section 43 becoming a regulatory loophole, particularly as some instruments are used both in investment business and in the wholesale markets.

Prior to the FSA, the Bank exercised informal authority over the traditional foreign exchange, bullion and money markets, and monitored the development of markets in related derivatives such as FRAs, futures, options and swaps. Following the FSA, the Bank developed a formal (but non-statutory) wholesale markets supervision regime under a special *Wholesale Markets Supervision Division* (separate from its Banking Supervision Division). The regime was elaborated upon in the so-called *Grey Book*, formally entitled *The Regulation of the Wholesale Markets in Sterling, Foreign Exchange and Bullion*, which was published by the Bank in April 1988 (and updated June 1992). The wholesale markets supervision regime can be broadly divided into two functions:

- *designation* of institutions eligible for exemption from the FSA under Section 43 and for supervision by the Bank of England (Chapter I of the *Grey Book)*;

- *conduct of business rules* (Chapter II of the *Grey Book*):
  - capital adequacy requirements:
  - the London Code of Conduct.

Designation for exemption from the FSA

No institution can be unconditionally exempted from the FSA, given the diversity of instruments traded by most financial institutions. Some instruments traded in the wholesale market are also defined as investments by the FSA.

Exemption from the FSA is therefore limited to *particular* transactions. The Bank of England developed a set of criteria to distinguish when transactions are wholesale (and therefore eligible for exemption from the FSA). The transactional criteria are twofold:

- identity of *instrument*;

- *size* of transaction.

The Bank offered three categories of transaction based on its two criteria:

- transactions in **wholesale designated** instruments, which are all exempted from the FSA on the assumption that the type of institution transacting will automatically be wholesale and which are:
  - sterling wholesale deposits
  - foreign currency wholesale deposits
  - spot and forward foreign exchange
  - spot and forward gold and silver bullion
  - commercial bills

- transactions in **investment designated** instruments, which are listed in the table below, for which exemption from the FSA depends on the *size* of the transaction:

instrument	minimum transaction size (£)
London CDs	100,000
commercial paper	100,000
short-term non-London CDs	100,000
other short-term debentures	100,000
local authority debt	100,000
short-term public sector debt	100,000
OTC currency options	500,000
OTC interest rate options	500,000
gold and silver options	500,000
FRAs	500,000
SAFEs (ERAs and FXAs)	500,000
interest rate swaps	500,000
currency swaps	500,000
repos	100,000

Using the criteria above, the Bank of England clarifies *institutions* for the purpose of judging eligibility for exemption from the FSA into:

- **listed institutions** — specifically listed by the Bank of England for exemption from the FSA as being 'fit and proper' (by reason of its capital, management and operational resources, standards of business conduct, and high reputation and standing) to act on a regular basis as either *market-makers* or *brokers* in one or more wholesale-designated instruments; listed institutions have no protection as investors under the FSA for any transactions in wholesale designated instruments;

■ **wholesale market counterparties** — unlisted institutions having undertaken transactions in wholesale-designated instruments and in amounts recognised by the Bank of England as wholesale and within the previous 18 months: these institutions have very little protection for investors under the FSA for transactions in wholesale-designated instruments or in investments designated instruments in wholesale amounts;

■ **investment customers** — unlisted institutions transacting wholesale-designated instruments, but not in wholesale amounts; or listed or unlisted institutions transacting investment-designated instruments or undesignated instruments, whatever the amount: these institutions have considerable protection as investors under the FSA.

London Code of Conduct

The Bank of England's revised *Grey Book* of May 1992 formally entitled *The London Code of Conduct: a guide to best practice in the wholesale money markets*, sets out Codes of Conduct for (1) the 'traditional' sterling money market, (2) swaps, (3) bullion, (4) foreign currency assets and (5) other wholesale markets. The sections specifically concerning interest rate swaps are:

■ *Deals at non-current rates* (page 4). As a general rule, the Bank cautions against the use of off-market rates. It accepts their use in swaps, but advises that management should be satisfied that proper controls are in place to ensure that off-market rates do not create unexceptable conflict of interest, are not used to conceal illegal activities and that the overall terms of off-market swaps (including fee payments) should be in line with par swaps.

■ *Know your customer* (page 4). When entering into transactions in swaps, the Bank recommends as good practice the sending of pre-deal telexes to inexperienced counterparties outlining key terms and strongly recommends the preparation of checklists for use when negotiating and finalising arrangements for swaps. A sample checklist is provided (this was set out in *Part Three*).

■ *Procedures: firmness of quotation* (page 5). The Bank notes that considerable use is made in the swap market of 'indicative interest' quotations and that an unconditional firm price is only to be given where a principal intermediary deals directly with a counterparty or when such a principal has received the name of a counterparty from a broker. It states that a principal who quotes a price as 'firm subject to credit' is bound to deal at that price if the counterparty is in a category of counterparty previously identified as acceptable for this purpose. The only exception is where an intermediary has reached its credit limit for a counterparty. It is not acceptable practice to revise a price which was 'firm subject to credit' once the counterparty has been named. Brokers and principal intermediaries are advised to establish ranges of institutions for which prices quoted to brokers are firm subject to credit.

■ *Terms and documentation* (page 8). The Bank encourages the use of standard terms and conditions such as BBAIRS and ISDA Interest Rate and Currency Exchange Agreements. In the case of the latter, the Bank advises that all material options and/or modifications allowed for in Schedule A, and/or choices offered via the Interest Rate and Currency Exchange Definitions, must be clearly stated before dealing. Firms should make clear at an early stage if they are not intending to use standard terms and where changes are proposed. In swaps, the Bank argues that institutions should treat themselves as bound to a deal at the point where the commercial terms of the transactions are agreed and that making swap transactions subject to agreement on documentation is not best practice. It states that counterparties must make every effort to progress the finalisation of documentation. The Bank believes it should be possible for this to be accomplished within two months of the deal being struck and regards longer than three months as excessive.

■ *Assignments or transfers* (page 8). Counterparties which enter into a swap with the intention of shortly afterwards assigning the deal to a third party are advised to make clear their intention to do so when initially negotiating the deal. It is also recommended that the confirmation sent by counterparties should specify any intent to assign and give details of the procedure that will be used. The subsequent documentation should also make provision for assignment. Consent for the assignment must be secured from the other counterparty before releasing its name to the third party. The other counterparty is obliged to provide sufficient information to enable the assignment to be conducted in accordance with other provisions of the Code, in particular, details of the type of credit acceptable as a new counterparty and reimbursements required to cover administrative costs. Finally, it is noted that proper and clear documentation is just as important for the assignment of swaps as for their origination.

Self-Study Exercises: <u>Questions</u>   Part 5

Question 5.1:   What is the normal measure of the current credit risk on an interest rate swap?

Question 5.2:   How is the normal measure of current credit risk, which was the subject of Question 5.1, measured arithmetically?

Question 5.3:   How is the replacement swap normally priced?

Question 5.4:   How is *netting* supposed to reduce credit risk?

Question 5.5:   What is the minimum risk capital required under the Basle Agreement for a coupon swap with an OECD-based private sector counterparty which has a notional principal amount of £45m with six years remaining to maturity using the *original exposure method*?

Self-Study Exercises: <u>Answers</u>   Part 5

Answer 5.1:   Credit risk on interest rate swaps is normally measured in terms of the *replacement cost* of the swap in the event of default by the counterparty to the swap. As swap rates will have almost certainly changed between the negotiation of the swap and the default, the replacement swap will cost more or less than the original swap. Any increase in cost measures credit risk.

Answer 5.2:   Normally, replacement cost is measured solely in terms of the difference between the swap rates of the original and replacement swaps ie, fixed interest rates. Any differences in floating interest rates are usually ignored: because floating interest rates are reset periodically and frequently, it is assumed that a replacement swap will not represent much of a disturbance to the floating interest cash flow (however, this is not always true).

Answer 5.3:   Normally, a replacement swap is priced at the price of the original swap and any difference between the original and current swap rates is settled by means of a cash payment between the counterparties to the replacement swap. For example, if the current swap rate is above the original swap rate, the receiver of fixed interest through a replacement swap should be compensated by a cash payment for sub-market rate of interest received through the swap.

Answer 5.4:   Netting should reduce credit risk by allowing a creditor counterparty having several swaps outstanding with a defaulting counterparty to net off the value of swaps with positive values against the value of swaps with a negative value, thereby reducing its overall loss in the event of default.

Answer 5.5:   An interest rate swap with an OECD-based private-sector counterparty has credit risk weighting under the Basle Agreement of 50% of its NPA. The swap in Question 5.5 has an NPA of £45m and thus a credit risk-weighted exposure of £22.5m. Under the original exposure method, 1% of the credit risk-weighted exposure is regarded at risk for remaining maturities of 1-2 years plus 1% for each extra year. The swap in Question 5.5 has six years remaining to maturity and thus 5% (1% for the first two years and 1% for each of the remaining years). The overall exposure is therefore 5% of 50% of £45m, which is £1,125,000. Of this, a minimum of 8% is required as risk capital, which is £90,000.

Glossary

All-in price

The price of an interest rate swap quoted as an absolute percentage rate of interest. Generally used for *money market swaps*. The alternative is to quote the price of a swap in terms of a *spread* over a benchmark yield.

Arranger

An intermediary which arranges a swap between two end-users without actually directly participating in the transaction. An arranger performs the same function as a *broker*, but it differs in that it is normally a principal counterparty. Arrangers charge fees rather than take a dealing spread.

As of basis

The documentation for interest rate swaps is often exchanged after confirmations. Such deals are said to have been made on an *as of* basis.

Asset swap

An interest rate swap which exchanges interest received on assets.

Assignment

The sale of an interest rate swap by one of the counterparties (the assignor) to a third party (the assignee). The assignee effectively substitutes for the assignor. Assignment requires the agreement of the other counterparty. The value of the swap is exchanged between the assignor and the assignee in a cash payment.

Basis swap

An interest rate swap between two streams of interest payments, each calculated using a different floating interest rate index. Also known as an *index swap*.

BBAIRS

British Bankers' Association Interest Rate Swap: applied to the BBA's *Recommended Terms and Conditions for London Interbank Interest Rate Swaps*; and to the *Interest Settlement Rate* published daily on behalf of the BBA by *Telerate* on screen pages 3740-50 for use in resetting the floating interest rate in swaps in several major currencies, for a range of tenors between 1 and 12 months.

Broker

An intermediary which arranges swaps between end-users without actually directly participating in the transaction. Brokers perform the same function as *arrangers*, but differ in that they specialise in arrangement. Brokers charge fees related to the size of the swap rather than taking dealing spreads between transaction prices: this is to ensure that they are impartial between the swap counterparties in terms of price and are interested only in matching two counterparties at mutually satisfactory terms so that a deal is consummated.

Buyer

In a *coupon swap*, the buyer is the counterparty paying fixed interest and is therefore also known as the *payer*.

Cherry-picking

The action of the receiver or administrator of a swap counterparty which is bankrupt or in administration in maintaining swap contracts with a counterparty which are still profitable, while defaulting on those with the same counterparty which are not.

Coupon swap

An interest rate swap between two streams of interest payments, where one is calculated using an interest rate fixed for the life of the swap and the other is calculated using a floating interest rate. In other words, a fixed-against-floating interest rate swap.

Generic swap

An interest rate swap which has:

— constant *notional principal amount*;

— exchange of fixed and floating interest (ie, a *coupon swap*);

— constant fixed interest rate;

— floating interest rate with no margin;

— regular (but not necessarily simultaneous) payments of fixed and floating interest;

— immediate or spot start;

— no special risk features.

IMM swap

A money market interest rate swap which coincides precisely with the contract periods for the three-month Eurodollar futures contracts traded on the *International Monetary Market (IMM)*, a division of the *Chicago Mercantile Exchange (CME)*. This allows hedging and arbitraging between swaps and futures without basis risk due to differences in maturity.

Index swap

A *basis swap*.

Interest rate swap

A contract which commits two counterparties to exchange, over an agreed period, two streams of interest payments, each calculated using a different interest rate index, but applied to a common *notional principal amount*.

ISDA

International Swap Dealers' Association. A New York-based organisation, established in March 1985, representing market-makers in interest rate and cross-currency swaps. Its most tangible achievement has been the production of standardised contract documentation for swaps.

Market-maker

An intermediary which is committed to quote firm buying and selling (two-way) prices for swaps in all trading conditions.

Marking to market

Revaluing swaps and other instruments by calculating the profit or loss which would be required if a replacement instrument had to be transacted at current market prices.

Master contract

A document which sets out standard terms and conditions for a swap transaction and only has to be updated with details specific to a new transaction, such as price, maturity, notional principal amount, etc. This allows dealers to avoid lengthy and complex negotiations for simple swaps, by limiting agreement to a few key details. Other terms and conditions are settled by reference to the master contract. The master contracts drafted by *ISDA* work by novation: each new deal is added as an appendix to the master contract and becomes part of a single integrated contract, together with all previous deals under the master contract. This technique is intended to assist in enforcing the netting of swaps in the event of a default.

Money market swap

A swap, usually with an original tenor of two or three years. Money market swaps are priced from futures contracts. As opposed to a *term swap*.

Netting

In the event of default by a swap counterparty, the ability of individual creditors to offset the value of outstanding swaps which are profitable to the defaulter against the value of swaps which are unprofitable to it. This reduces the loss in the event of default by an active user of swaps by avoiding *cherry-picking*.

New issue arbitrage

Arbitrage between a new borrowing (typically a Eurobond issue) and an interest rate swap. Where such an arbitrage opportunity exists, the borrower will receive fixed interest through the swap at a rate higher than it pays on its borrowing and end up paying subsidised floating interest. If the borrower has borrowed floating interest, it will pay fixed interest through the swap at a rate much lower than its direct cost of borrowing fixed interest and end up paying subsidised fixed interest.

Notional principal amount

The amount of principal which is used to calculate the interest to be exchanged through an interest rate swap from the interest rates in terms of which the swap is priced. In a single-currency interest rate swap, there is no exchange of principal.

Off-market

A swap which is priced at other than a current market rate.

Par

A swap which is priced at a current market rate.

Payer

In a *coupon swap*, the payer is the counterparty paying fixed interest and is also known as the *buyer*.

Price

In a *coupon swap*, because the convention is to assume a standard floating interest rate index (usually six-month Libor), swaps are quoted in terms of the fixed interest rate only.

Receiver

In a *coupon swap*, the receiver is the counterparty receiving fixed interest and is also known as the *seller*.

Replacement cost

The difference between the net present value of an existing swap and the net present value of a new swap at a current market rate. The amount which would be gained or lost if the counterparty to the existing swap defaulted and the other counterparty negotiated a new replacement swap. The usual measure of the current credit risk on an interest rate swap.

Reverse

A new interest rate swap which is opposite to an existing swap in terms of the direction of interest payments and acts as a hedge against the impact of further interest rate changes. Also called a matching swap.

Seller

In a *coupon swap*, the seller is the counterparty receiving fixed interest and is therefore also known as the *receiver*.

Strip

The average interest rate on a series of consecutive FRAs and interest rate futures. *Money market swap* rates are strips of FRAs or futures.

Synthetic

By putting on a *coupon swap* through which they pay fixed interest, a fixed-interest investor ends up receiving net floating interest and a floating-interest borrower ends up paying net fixed interest. By putting on a coupon swap through which they receive fixed interest, a floating-interest investor ends up receiving net fixed interest and a fixed-interest borrower ends up paying net floating interest. Because the original assets and liabilities remain on the balance sheet, but their interest rate basis changes, swaps are said to have synthesized new instruments from old.

Swap spread

The difference between the *all-in* price of a swap and a benchmark yield (usually the yield on a government security). *Term swaps* in major currencies are normally quoted as swap spreads. When a swap is agreed, the swap spread and benchmark yield are fixed, and an all-in price calculated.

Termination

The cancellation of a swap contract. One counterparty pays the other the value of the swap as a cash payment to compensate for the loss of expected profit over the remainder of the life of the swap.

Term swap

A swap with a remaining period to maturity of more than two or three years. As opposed to *money market swaps*.

Warehousing

The temporary hedging of interest rate swaps until a matching or *reverse* swap can be agreed. Warehousing usually involves the buying or selling short of government fixed-interest securities. For example, the *payer* of fixed interest through a swap would warehouse by buying such securities. If interest rates fell — which would mean that a matching swap would pay less fixed interest than is being paid out on its existing swap — the price of the securities would increase and compensate for the loss on the swaps.

How to mark the self-study questions

Each of the questions has been awarded between 1 and 11 marks. The marks are set out in the table. Where questions have more than one part, fractions can be awarded. When all the marks have been added up, the results should be asessed against the distribution curve below.

Question	Part one	Part two	Part three	Part four	Part five
1	1	1	2.5	1	1
2	1	1	1	4	2
3	1	1	2	5	2
4	1	1	2	5	1
5	1	1	2	5	4
6	1	1	2		
7	1	1	2		
8	1	1	1		
9	1	1	4		
10	1	2	1.5		
11		2			
12		2			
13		2			
14		5			
15		5			
16		5			
17		1			
18		1			
19		3			
20		3			
Total	**10**	**40**	**20**	**20**	**10**

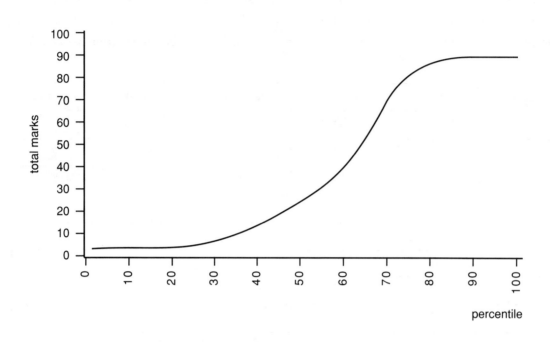

Percentile	Assessment
0—50%	You should start the Workbook again. Check that you work through it more methodically than before and in an environment conducive to study.
50—60%	You should think about re-reading the Workbook to reinforce your understanding of swaps. If you have lost marks in just one or two chapters, there is probably no need to re-read the whole Workbook, but you should go through the worked answers with care.
60—80%	A good result. You should think about skimming through the Workbook again to consolidate your knowledge.
80—100%	An excellent result. You should be able to progress quite easily to more specialised texts on swaps.

Coopers & Lybrand offices

Australia
D Prothero
Coopers & Lybrand Tower
580 George Street Sydney
New South Wales 2000
Tel: (03) 606 4500

Austria
H Wirth
Postfach 161
A 1092
Vienna
Tel: (1) 31377 0

Bahamas
C Johnson
PO Box N 596
Nassau NP
Tel: (809) 322 1061

Bahrain
F Ruttonsha
PO Box 787
Manama
Tel: (0973) 53007

Belgium
R Eeckhout
Marcel Thirty Court
Avenue Marcel Thirty 216
B-1200 Brussels
Tel: (02) 774 42 11

Bermuda
G Holmes
PO Box HM1171
Hamilton
Bermuda HMEX
Tel: (809) 295 2000

Brazil
P Baraldi
Caixa Postal 3168
CEP 01060
Sao Paulo
SP Brazil
Tel: (11) 530 0200

Canada
David Atkins
Aetna Canada Centre
145 King Street West
Toronto
Ontario
M5H 1V8
Tel: (416) 869 1130

Channel Islands
J Horrell
La Motte Chambers
St Helier
Jersey
Tel: (0534) 602000

Cyprus
D Papadopoulos
PO Box 1612
Nicosia
Tel: (02) 453053

Denmark
K Villadsen
PO Box 1443
DK 7500
Holstebro
Tel: (97-42) 19 88

Finland
M Tervo
PL 1015
00101
Helsinki
Tel: (0) 658 044

France
K Pilgrem
BP 451-08
75366 Paris
Cedex 08
Tel: (1) 44 20 80 00

Germany
H Wagener
Treuarbeit AG
Postfach 120
D-W 1000
Berlin 15
Tel: (030) 884 2020

Germany
K Lührig
Truehand-Vereiningung AG
Postfach 170 552
D-W 6000
Frankfurt am Main 1
Tel: (069) 71100

Hong Kong
R Chalmers
Sunning Plaza
10 Hysan Avenue
Hong Kong
Tel: 839 4321

Hungary
A Romer-Lee
PO Box 694
1539 Budapest
Tel: (1) 135 0140

Isle of Man
C Talavera
12 Finch Road
Douglas
Tel: (0624) 626711

Italy
P Barone
Via del Quirinale
00187 Rome
Tel: (0) 6 4744896

Japan
N Yamakoshi
Shin-Aoyama Bldg
Twin West 20F
1-1 Minami Aoyama 1-Chome
Minato-Ku
Tokyo 107
Tel: (3) 3475 1722

Leichtenstein
R Silvani
PO Box 1113
9490 Vaduz
Tel: 2 90 80

Luxembourg
M Chèvremont
BP 1446
L-1014
Luxembourg
Tel: 49749 1

Malaysia
M Abdullah
PO Box 10184
50706
Kuala Lumpur
Tel: (3) 441 1188

Malta
J Bonello
PO Box 61
Valleta Malta
Tel: 233648

Mexico
H Lara Silva
Apartado Postal 24-348
Col Roma
06700 Mexico
DF
Tel: (5) 208 1277

Netherlands
H Schaper
PO Bix 4200
1009 AE
Amsterdam
Tel: (20) 568 6666

New Zealand
R Hill
GPO Box 243
Wellington 6000
Tel: (4) 499 9898

Norway
E Westerby
Havnelageret
0150 Oslo 1
Tel: 02 40 00 00

Poland
D Thomas
Iwonicka 19
09-924 Warsaw
Tel: (22) 42 87 66

Portugal
C Bernardes
PO Box 1910
1004 Lisbon Codex
Tel: 793 0023

Rep of Ireland
B Cunningham
PO Box 1283
Dublin 2
Tel: (01) 610333

Rep of South Africa
R Barrow
PO Box 2536
Johannesburg 2000
Tel: (011) 498 4000

Russia
S Root
Ulinska Schchepkina 6
Moscow 129090
Tel: (095) 281 9466

Saudi Arabia
G Karaman
PO Box 2762
Riyad 11461
Tel: (01) 477 9504

Singapore
D Compton
Orchard PO Box 285
Singapore 9123
Tel: 336 2344

Spain
JJ Hierro
Apartado de Correos
36-191
28080 Madrid
Tel: (1) 572 0233

Sultanate of Oman
N Ferrand
PO Box 6075
Ruwi
Tel: 5637 17

Sweden
Johan Hafstrom
PO Box 27318
S-102 54 Stockholm
Tel: (8) 666 8000

Switzerland
R. Tschudi
Postfach 4152
CH 4002
Basel
(060) 277 5500

Thailand
N Charoentaveesub
GPO Box 788
Bangkok 10501
Tel: (2) 236 5227 9

Turkey
M Clarke
Buyukdere cad No 111
Kat; 2-3
Istanbul
Tel: (1) 175 2840

United Arab Emirates
H Nehme
PO Box 990
Abu Dhabi
Gayrettepe 80300
Tel: (02) 21123

United Kingdom
P. Reyniers
P.Rivett
London EC4A 4HT
Tel: (071) 583 5000

United States of America
C Jenkins
One Post Office Square
Boston
Massachusetts 02109
Tel: (617) 7574 5000

United States of America
W Van Rijn
1301 Avenue of the Americas
New York
NY 10019-6013
Tel: 259 7000